# FOREWORD

As one who loves Virginia — every mountain, every valley, every seashore — and who has been many times to every nook and corner of our state, I am delighted to share this new book with the leisure traveler, whether a fellow Virginian or a visitor. *Bed & Breakfast and Unique Inns of Virginia* portrays the history, beauty, character and hospitality that embody the Old Dominion.

The photographs alone entice one to explore unknown corners of our diverse state. Michael and Bruce Muncy have spent a year capturing on film the quiet charm that still surrounds our many cities and towns, neighborhoods and countryside. Not everything has gone high tech. And that is precisely the charisma of Virginia's more than 300 bed & breakfasts and inns — you step back into time from the pressures of modern-day life and have a chance to relive the spirit of bygone eras.

Virginia started it all, with the founding of Jamestown, the first permanent English settlement in 1607. Thus, Virginia's rich history dates back nearly 400 years. Some of its many old fine homes have been converted into the inns recorded in this book.

Virginia has it all. The ocean, bay, rivers and trickling creeks. The Piedmont region of peanuts, country ham, horses and hunts. The Shenandoah Valley. The coal fields of the Southwest. The Eastern Shore. And, of course, the mountains, the beloved mountains.

Among our priceless treasures are the Skyline Drive and Blue Ridge Parkway that wind their way across most of Virginia down into North Carolina. One of my greatest pleasures is hiking up Old Rag Mountain and enjoying the wonderful, natural resources so abundant throughout the state.

It was our mutual appreciation of the Blue Ridge Parkway that first caused my path to cross with Lynn Davis, the author. We worked on the Parkway's 1985 Golden Anniversary and 1987 Dedication, memorable events that focused national attention on America's popular roadway, also one of Virginia's premier attractions.

When I chaired Virginia's economic development program in the early 1960's, I learned to appreciate the importance of tourism to our state: it means jobs and an enhanced tax base.

Tourists now spend over $5.5 billion here — making tourism the second largest industry in the state. These figures do not happen by accident. There is an enormous amount of things to see and do here. Our heritage is rich. You will find that Virginia's bed and breakfasts reflect just that.

I enthusiastically commend this book to you. The love the photographers, author, innkeepers and I have for the Commonwealth of Virginia is gently revealed here. You will come to share our feeling as you travel the historic routes and scenic byways. The memories of old will become your memories.

Harry F. Byrd, Jr.
United States Senator 1965 - 83

dedicated to
our families and especially our children —
Cameron Cullop, Lee Cullop, Sara Muncy, Brian Muncy,
Jason Davis —
for their patience, love, understanding,
support and prayers

*"There is one thing that gives radiance to everything and that is the possibility of something around the corner."*

G. K. Chesterton, English essayist

# BED & BREAKFAST and UNIQUE INNS of VIRGINIA

Photography by Bruce & Michael Muncy
Text by Lynn Davis

Foreword by Senator Harry F. Byrd, Jr.

CRYSTAL SPRINGS

PUBLISHING

**Bed & Breakfast and Unique Inns of Virginia.**
Copyright © 1988 by Crystal Springs Publishing. Printed and bound in the United States of America. All rights reserved. No part of this book may be reproduced in any form or by any electronic or mechanical means including information storage and retrieval systems without permission in writing from the publisher, except by a reviewer, who may quote brief passages in a review. Published by Crystal Springs Publishing, P.O. Box 8814, 3030 Burnleigh Rd., Roanoke, VA 24014.

First Printing 1988

Library of Congress Catalog
Card Number 88-072026
ISBN: 0-9620996-0-0

**Cover: Designed by Dianne Smith**

Photographs

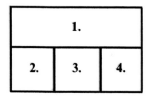

1. Inn at Narrow Passage
2., 3. Clifton
4. Martha Washington Inn

# ABOUT THE AUTHORS

### Bruce Muncy

. . . a gentle perfectionist at his art of photography.

Bruce owns a commercial photography business in Roanoke, Va., which produces architectural photography, product illustration and portraits. He is the only photographer in Roanoke to have earned the coveted *Master of Photography* and *Photographic Craftsman* degrees presented by the Professional Photographers of America (P.P.A.). He is the youngest recipient and the sole photographer in the State of Virginia to be named *Associate* by the American Society of Photographers. This honor has been presented to just 28 photographers in America. He is the only commercial photographer in Virginia to be selected as a commercial/industrial juror on the P.P.A.'s approved affiliate juror list. For two years in a row he has been awarded the *Kodak Award of Excellence*, Virginia's highest photographic award. Well-known throughout the East and Mid-West, he has received countless other awards and has spoken at numerous conventions and institutes. His dedication to professional excellence has been lauded by his peers.

### Michael Muncy

. . . a vibrant, spirited personality who can capture nature's most exquisite images on film.

Michael is an award-winning photographer known for her high quality, nature images. The outdoors is the source for her inspiration and creativity. She happens to be Bruce's wife, his photographic assistant and the company's sales representative. Michael is a native Virginian and a distant cousin of Robert E. Lee. Her award-winning wall decor and photographs are displayed in offices and private residences throughout several states. Among her many plaudits are several *Court of Honor* awards for best of the blue ribbon winners in Virginia. Some of her works are included in an international traveling exposition of the Professional Photographers of America.

### Lynn Davis

. . . a Virginian by birth, a traveler by love, with a Renaissance view of life.

Lynn, a writer, editor, designer and erstwhile photographer, has also won numerous state and national awards for her work, including a *Newsweek* award for a University of Maryland newsmagazine and a first place from the Printing Industries of the Virginias for her *Roanoke Valley* book for the Roanoke Valley Chamber of Commerce. She has judged numerous national publications contests and given various journalism seminars. In the early days of her career she interned at one of Washington, D.C.'s largest "inns" and wrote travel articles for the Baltimore-Washington International Airport. She has worked with the Virginia Division of Tourism on projects and most recently completed highly successful media campaigns for the Blue Ridge Parkway 50th Anniversary and Dedication. Family visits have taken her up and down the Shenandoah Valley hundreds of times. She has combed the Commonwealth point to point by car, motorcycle, airplane, bicycle, foot, horse, mule, canoe and other floating devices.

# ACKNOWLEDGMENTS

**Bed & Breakfast and Unique Inns of Virginia** was a team effort by Virginians. This book about Virginia was "Made in Virginia," and we are especially proud of the fact that it reflects the work of professionals from the beautiful Roanoke Valley, an area filled with a surprising abundance of talent. Our many heartfelt thanks to everyone who helped.

Calligraphy: Dianne Smith, Artist

Color Separations: Roanoke Engraving
    Boyd C. Ayers, Proofer
    David Mikula, Scanner Operator
    Tony Waller, President

Cover Design: Dianne Smith, Artist
    Lynn Davis
    Bruce and Michael Muncy

Film Processing: Kessler Color Lab
    Rudder Photo Lab

Paper: Dillard Paper Company
    Lisa Lavery, Sales Promotion
        Representative
        (80 lb. LOE Gloss Text,
        12 pt. Cast Coated Cover)

Printing: Progress Press, Inc.
    Thelma Adams, Prepress
    Robert Chocklett, Treasurer
    Marion Dickenson, Typesetter
    Sandy Dooley, Typesetter
    Jamie Greenwood, Prepress
    Buddy Hogan, Prepress Supervisor
    Hazel Shockley, Proofreader
    Jimmy Smith, Pressman
    Lucille Wallace, Proofreader
    Wiley Wright, Estimator/Planner

Promotions: Lin Chaff Public Relations
    Lynn Davis
    Bruce and Michael Muncy

Proofreading: Amanda Aikman
    Emily Brady
    Nina Matthews
    Ina McDonald

Publishing Office:
    Charlotte Bradley, Secretary

Text Design/Graphic Production:
    Ann Hyde, Design Publish Plus
    Lynn Davis
    Bruce and Michael Muncy

# TABLE OF CONTENTS

# BED & BREAKFAST
### and Unique Inns of Virginia

Welcome to the wonderful world of Virginia's B&B's and unique inns! Where . . .

- Almost everything is antique and often for sale, even the bed you sleep on.
- Dining takes place in a gristmill and guests select their own wines from the cellar while watching the cogs of the waterwheel.
- A 1600-acre wildlife preserve with boarding even for your horses, and two miles of sterling trout stream await you.
- Aristocratic settings merit porches that are called verandas and gardens yield such a productive harvest that the hosts encourage you to pick your own vegetables.
- A sprawling, restored Victorian home is replete with a spiral staircase, an aviary and a brick kiln furnace converted to house guinea pigs for sale.

We cannot talk about bed and breakfast homes without being personal, because their very essence embodies an intimate hospitality. Preserving a heritage rich in tradition and history, the B&B's and inns serve travelers who want a personal touch in their accommodations, a homey respite while on the road, an escape from occupational pressures and busy lifestyles to tranquility, rest and comfort.

Our book is more than a pictorial guide. It hobnobs with the innkeepers and hosts themselves. It echoes Virginia's past and is riveted with a rainbow of adventures to be had and places to see in the Old Dominion. It celebrates the modern version of innkeeping and zooms in on the proud vestiges of bygone eras. Indeed, B&B's are like a diamond in today's world of fakes.

If you cherish fine art, authentic antiques, classy decor, interesting architecture, creative styles and good eating, then you're a prime candidate for becoming the next B&B convert. If you've grown disenchanted with the predictability and monotony of motel chains, then B&B's offer you an alluring alternative.

A place to come apart, they are reminiscent of a quaint lifestyle. You do not need to come with an agenda: you can just cruise on R&R control. If energy injects your veins, you will discover that most B&B's nest in small towns or rural settings near a variety of historical sites, antique shops, folk art and craft stores, country cuisine and outdoor pleasures.

Inn hopping is a grand way to sightsee because you get to know an area best through its residents. Many of the pedigreed homes themselves are steeped in history, rich with the memories of famous people and heroic events. They are a goldmine of antiques.

Inn hopping is also a masterful way to collect recipes, restoration tips and decorating ideas, as well as learn the B&B business to open one yourself.

Perhaps the heartwarming appeal of B&B's comes from the feeling that you are living the way your ancestors used to. You recall the halcyon days when you made trips to your grandparents' home — nostalgia imprinted forever in your mind.

Whatever the attraction, B&B's are experiencing dynamic popularity, especially with the sophisticated traveler. Virginia has well over 300 B&B's throughout the state, with the Charlottesville area alone a mecca for 100. The quiet revolution underway in America's vacation lodging industry is evidenced by the rapid proliferation of B&B's, 10,000 strong across the land and more hanging out their shingles daily.

The floodgates may have opened up for aesthetic reasons. City dwellers longing for a haven from rush hour traffic and the surly demands of life on every second of their time, welcome a retreat to the quiet joys of nature. Leaving the flashy world of neon, high-pacers protect their sanity by getting away from it all. B&B's satisfy the appetite for a perfect weekend getaway.

You willingly trade the radios and stereos for the songbirds. Without highrises blocking your view, you can watch the glitter of a peach sun rising or setting. You relish sleepy afternoons amid romantic places of old, where you indulge in the simpler pleasures of life, preferring a canopied bed to a drink machine on every floor, sincere conversation to a cocktail lounge, a quiet street to an interstate. The liberal measure of ambience rekindles your spirit.

A cornerstone for European travelers since Medieval times, B&B lodging in a private home remains deeply rooted in Great Britain's culture. The colonists brought the concept with them, and down through the centuries Virginia inns served pioneers, patriots, future presidents, businessmen, Civil War troops, and tourists, especially those traveling to the spas that were so fashionable in the 1800s. In today's B&B revival American entrepreneurs still emulate the English estates and manor houses catering to travelers.

Many B&B's are converted old buildings or modern versions of traditional inns. Their offerings range from a small, one bedroom to a full service inn. Some are homey, some posh, modestly priced to expensive. Many offer the peace and solitude of the country wayside, mountaintop or riverfront. Others reside in the heart of downtown historic districts, where city lights and lively nights are the rule. Some are staked close to Washington, D.C.; others hibernate in remote little valleys or lovely country villages of the Allegheny and Blue Ridge mountains. The selection is diverse, no two alike.

Every B&B has its distinguishing characteristics. Many hold historical significance and are museum quality. You see architectural detail you won't find in homes today, accompanied by the patrician grace of high ceilinged parlors, silver tea service, rose bouquets in the shadows of period furniture. You hear the creaks and groans of old hardwood floors against unsquared walls. You see some vintage plumbing.

B&B travel provides you with a glimpse into some of the most prestigious houses in Virginia. Quiet elegance starting at the doorstep. These homes offer such luxurious amenities as swimming pools, tennis courts, jacuzzies, bathrobes and bed turndown service.

Phil Irvin, innkeeper at Caledonia Farm affirms, "every B&B, just like caves, displays a different personality. You meet real people. The service is personal. And you are a special guest."

At times you may be the only guest, as we found out during visits of the 55 establishments pictured in our book. They all are scrupulously clean and first class, with something unique to offer — truly reflecting the style and personalities of the innkeepers.

The hosts open their homes because they genuinely enjoy company and like people. Affable, sociable and intelligent, innkeepers balance friendliness with respect for privacy. Most have traveled to some of the world's best B&B's for inspiration. They are dedicated to assuring your comfort, helping you plan your sightseeing or relax.

There are several ways to book rooms: contact the B&B directly (some interstate signs now list B&B's at a particular exit) or use a reservation service. The conscientious services screen the homes they represent and match guests to compatible lodging. Many homes are available only through reservation services, which receive their remuneration in the form of booking commissions. The index at the back of our book includes these services.

You ought to book three to four weeks in advance for popular regions. Certain peak seasons may require six to 12 months' prior booking. During the week you can usually get last minute booking. Most B&B's hold your reservation with an advance deposit. Make sure you ask in detail about the kind of accommodation you desire: private or shared bath, bath with tub or shower,

working fireplace in your room, if transportation is provided from airports or train stations, what sporting equipment is on the premises and if the charge is per room or per guest. In the back of our book the Cross Listing charts the specific amenities available. Tips are unnecessary, but innkeepers love thank you notes.

The hosts usually mingle with their guests and serve a continental breakfast often more substantial than advertised. Almost every innkeeper serves a special bread, and fruit is often included. Many hosts serve beverages to arriving guests, and some are gourmet cooks who conjure up regional specialties. Afternoon tea in the English tradition is a ritual at several B&B's.

There are hazy distinctions between the meanings of "inn" and "B&B." An inn is basically a commercial property with signs displayed to encourage direct booking. It has a long history of service and usually provides a major source of income to the proprietors, who often operate restaurants that serve a full range of meals to the public as well as to overnight guests. They tend to be somewhat less personal than B&B's.

A "B&B" is usually an owner-occupied house with up to six bedrooms and serves breakfast to overnight guests. Reservation services help travelers secure lodging primarily in these private homestays and guesthouses, rather than inns. Signs are not always displayed on the property. And the income derived from many B&B's usually does not represent the primary source of income. "Guesthouse," a term popular in the 1950s, is sometimes used in reference to today's upscaled B&B version. Some inns, however, even though they have over six rooms, operate more as a B&B.

If you are fresh off the motel circuit, you may have to make an adjustment to the personal nature of B&B's — they are not always completely private: you may have to share a bathroom, hotel services such as bellhops or room ser-

vice are missing, not all rooms have telephones or TV's, and you may not be able to arrive at any hour of the day or night. The one request that innkeepers stress is that you call if you find your given arrival time changes; otherwise, your host is kept waiting.

Jack Coleman, a Renaissance man who has made the news because he labored as a prison guard and ditch-digger on sabbaticals when he presided over such venerable institutions as Haverford College and the Federal Reserve Bank of Philadelphia, has now taken up innkeeping in Vermont in his "search of the dignity of man."

Perhaps that's what B&B's are really about, an antithesis to big business. A home substitute where families can gather for reunions or to celebrate a momentous occasion. A good place to honeymoon, for couples to get away, for business travelers to personalize their day. An ideal situation for single travelers because it eliminates the lonesomeness of a hotel room, and casual breakfast conversation makes for a pleasant start of the next day. A relaxed way to travel and a chance to recapture a sense of the past. A niche where you are made to feel like a very special person.

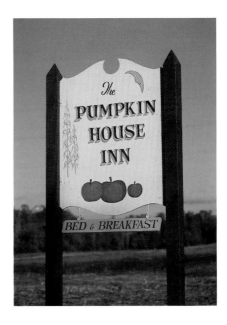

# The good Old Dominion, the blessed mother of us all — Thomas Jefferson

Ah — Virginia. No other place like it! Savor its offerings.

We may be city born and bred, but we all know the feeling of driving a narrow lane that rambles through the countryside of weathered barns and family homesteads — the place where America grew up. Come share the memories of Virginia. Come make memories.

America started with Jamestown. And in the ensuing years the "western" town of Fincastle sprang up. A land grant from the King of England gave it jurisdiction all the way to the Mississippi. Eight other states were formed from this territory: Illinois, Indiana, Kentucky, Michigan, Minnesota, Ohio, West Virginia and Wisconsin. Thus, Virginia is known as the "Mother of States." It is one of four commonwealth states, along with Kentucky, Massachusetts and Pennsylvania.

Virginia has also been nicknamed "Mother of Presidents" because eight U.S. presidents were born here: George Washington, Thomas Jefferson, James Madison, James Monroe, William Henry Harrison, John Tyler, Zachary Taylor and Woodrow Wilson. King Charles II called Virginia the Old Dominion because it remained loyal to the crown during the English Civil War of the mid-1600s.

Is it any wonder that the state of dogwoods, cardinals and foxhounds is a microcosm of all that went on before us? And that today it retains many historical treasures that give us insight into our past.

But its bounty does not stop with only historical landmarks. From the old world charm to its super beaches, romantic resorts, awesome beauty, outdoor recreation, and theme parks, Virginia has it all. The inns and B&B's make wonderful touring bases.

Virginia's heartland is finally proving the early German settlers and Thomas Jefferson right. The local soil, climate, modern viticulture and the *vitis vinifera* vines can produce superior grapes — placing the Old Dominion among the nation's top ten wine-producing states.

And only in Virginia do you have one of the Seven Wonders of the World, Natural Bridge. The Secretary of the Commonwealth designates three other natural wonders: Natural Chimneys; Natural Tunnels; and Luray Caverns, owned by Ted Graves, Virginia's father of modern tourism. Natural Tunnel, once called the Eighth Wonder of the World by William Jennings Bryan, is the remnant of a once larger cave in Duffield, the deep western part of the state in Scott County.

Off the beaten tracks are the Southwest Museum Historical State Park in Big Stone Gap, Smithfield Plantation (home of three Virginia governors) in Blacksburg, Shot Tower Historical Park outside of Wytheville, Red Hill Shrine at Brookneal (a little known but splendid tribute to Patrick Henry), the last capitol of the Confederacy in Danville, Chester Farms at Raphine, and Belle Grove Plantation in Middletown. From the coast to the mountains, like a marvelous patchwork quilt you come across an array of pleasures.

Hampton Roads encompasses Norfolk, Portsmouth, Chesapeake, Suffolk, Virginia Beach, Newport News and Hampton. A magnet for tourism and commerce, these communities converge where the James River, Chesapeake Bay and Atlantic Ocean meet.

Hampton is the oldest continuous English-speaking settlement in America. In addition to its historic district, visitors are enthralled with the NASA Langley Research Center, which trained the original astronauts. Cruise excursions will take you around the world's largest natural harbor and out into the Chesapeake Bay. The Kecoughtan Indian Village replicates a 17th-century Indian settlement.

Norfolk is being tagged these days as the city by the sea. Its revitalized skyline is a prize. Newport News is a world renowned shipbuilding center. A famed summer resort for many years, Virginia Beach has become the fastest growing city on the East Coast, as well as the largest city in Virginia. The Atlantic Ocean, however, is not the only attraction; the city's moderate climate averages 60.

The showcase of Williamsburg, between the York and James rivers, is its restored Colonial town. History buffs, however, also enjoy the other components of the Historic Triangle: Yorktown and Jamestown.

Mount Vernon in Fairfax County is one of Virginia's crown jewels, with more than a million visitors flocking to the Potomac River homestead 16 miles south of Washington. Except for the White House, it is the most visited historic home in the United States.

Gunston Hall, home of George Mason, who framed the Bill of Rights, and Woodlawn are also in Fairfax County, the Northern Virginia outlet to D.C. with the highest per capita income in the state.

Alexandria's Market Square features many outdoor festivals and programs. Old Town sports cobblestone streets and quaint historic townhouses that date back to the city's founding in 1749 by Scottish merchants.

Nearby Arlington features the Arlington National Cemetery and the Lee-Custis Mansion.

Out on what Virginians call the Northern Neck is Stratford Hall Plantation, whose claim to fame is that the only two brothers to sign the Declaration of Independence lived here: Richard Henry Lee and Francis Lightfoot Lee, father to Robert E. Lee. Neighboring Wakefield Plantation was George Washington's home until he reached four years of age.

Virginia's Eastern Shore, a 70-mile peninsula between the Atlantic Ocean and the Chesapeake Bay, is a refuge for more than 250 species of birds and wild ponies.

North of Fredericksburg, Warrenton lies in the middle of Virginia's hunt country. The Colonial tradition of foxhunting continues vibrantly, introduced in America by Washington and his employer-friend, Lord Fairfax.

Richmond, the capital city, combines the old and new. It is home to 15 Fortune 500 companies and ranks second in the South for having a record number of corporate headquarters. In existence since 1788, the State Capitol building is the second oldest working capitol in the United States. All the way to Williamsburg, the well-preserved James River plantations are in a category all by themselves. Some connoisseurs call Berkeley Plantation the most historic home in America; the first official Thanksgiving took place there. Area homes span 400 years.

North of Richmond rests Patrick Henry's home at Scotchtown and King's Dominion, theme park of fun. South of Richmond lies Hopewell, encrusted with 375 years of history. It nearly became the first permanent English settlement in the New World instead of Jamestown. Next door, Petersburg will keep you busy for a day.

At the foothills of the Blue Ridge, Charlottesville is Mr. Jefferson's country. Each year 500,000 visitors journey to Monticello, his classic home that was never completed. Tours of the University of Virginia are offered daily, beginning in the Rotunda. Polo matches take place most weekends from April to November.

In old Virginia the crossing of trails often determined the locations of towns. The Valley Pike, road of the 1700s, opened up the Shenandoah Valley. Western Virginia's earliest settlers were the German, Swiss and Scotch-Irish from Pennsylvania because the Blue Ridge Mountains served as a natural barrier to the English settlers of Jamestown for nearly 120 years.

The Blue Ridge on the east and the Alleghenies on the west carve out the beautiful Shenandoah Valley. Limestone caverns lace the underground, from Dixie Caverns west of Roanoke to those at the upper end: Skyline, Grand, Endless, Shenandoah, Massanutten, and Luray, dating back to its 1878 discovery.

The George Washington and Jefferson National Forests provide thousands of acres for wilderness delights. Shenandoah National Park covers 190,000 acres alone. The Skyline Drive and Blue Ridge Parkway yield a basketful of delights all their own; the scenic roadways are in sharp contrast to commercial highways. America's beloved Appalachian Trail chalks up more miles in Virginia than in any other state.

Travel brochures often quote the Indian legend that defines "Shenandoah" as "Daughter of the Stars," referring to the river running through the northern end of the valley. Some Parkway officials believe the word meant "spruce-lined mountain crest." Years ago before the ravages of time, pollution, or whatever, spruce trees apparently adorned the top of the Blue Ridge Mountains. Today only remnants are located atop Mt. Rogers and Whitetop not far from Abingdon.

Winchester, at the valley's upper end, is the oldest city west of the Blue Ridge. During the Civil War it changed hands no less than 72 times. It is a town of 18th century buildings, orchards filled with 700,000 trees, host of the Apple Blossom Festival each May, the old surveying headquarters of young Washington, his base in the French and Indian War, and the domain of one of Virginia's and America's greatest families, the Byrds. The city was home of the late Senator Harry F. Byrd Sr. and his brother, Rear Admiral Richard E. Byrd. Today Rosemont, Senator Byrd Jr.'s home, is open to the public with family memorabilia on display. Senator Byrd Sr. collaborated with President Franklin D. Roosevelt to get the Shenandoah National Park and Blue Ridge Parkway underway in 1932.

One of the newest museums on the scene is Staunton's Museum of American Frontier Culture, established to show how European farm traditions were adopted to fit the needs and resources of American settlers.

Lexington, another storehouse of history, reflects 19th century charm. Thomas "Stonewall" Jackson left his mark on Virginia Military Institute and Robert E. Lee his imprint on Washington and Lee University next door. The state's other newest attraction is located here, the Virginia Horse Center. A little further down the valley is the geological splendor of Natural Bridge, which draws 400,000 visitors yearly to gaze at the 90-foot-long arch of stone that bridges a 215-foot-deep gorge.

A third attraction new on the circuit is Poplar Forest, the octagonal home designed by Jefferson for his personal retreat between Bedford and Lynchburg.

Roanoke, the largest city along the Blue Ridge Parkway, is the economic hub of western Virginia. Blending urban and mountain cultures, Roanoke annually hosts the Miss Virginia Pageant and operates one of the oldest outdoor markets in the country. Its Center in the Square presents a dynamic concept of "culture under one roof": theatre, science museum, planetarium, fine arts museum, arts council and history museum.

Roanoke served as a key crossroads for the pioneers who pushed westward to America's frontier. Lewis and Clark, Sam Houston and Stephen Austin were from these parts. Sometime in the next few years the story that history books have skipped over will be told by the ambitious Explore Project. Roanoke visionaries are planning a new, regional attraction that will portray America's westward expansion from Roanoke to Cumberland Gap and westward.

South of Roanoke is Ferrum's Blue Ridge Museum and the Booker T. Washington National Monument, tribute to the leading black spokesman at the turn of the century.

Outdoor theaters relate the lore of western Virginia's rugged history. Mountain Lake, a marvelous old resort high in the sky, was the scene of the box office hit, *Dirty Dancing*. Abingdon's celebrated Barter Theater helped the likes of Noel Coward and Gregory Peck get started. Old Timey music can still be heard at the Galax Fiddlers' Convention each August.

The Grayson Highlands — an unheralded secret that can't stay quiet forever — offer a paradise to backpackers, cross country skiers, horseback riders, and anyone with a love of the outdoors.

Noblesse oblige — Virginians do what is expected of them. Robert E. Lee perhaps epitomized that to the nth degree. And Virginians do relish history. They have a saying:

*To be a Virginian, either by birth, marriage, adoption, or even on one's mother's side, is an introduction and a benediction from the Almighty God.*

# MARTHA WASHINGTON INN

*Supremely Elegant*

When this grand lady of Western Virginia was resurrected several years ago from dilapidation, the new owners, the United Company, spared no expense. Today it stands as a showpiece of grandeur. Travel the south over and you aren't likely to find more elegant hospitality anywhere, guests claim.

The magnificently restored hotel has a colorful past. Built in 1832 by Gen. Francis Preston and his wife, Sara Buchanan Preston (prominent figures in Virginian history), as their private residence, the mansion was sold in 1858 and made a Methodist College. It survived the Civil War, during which time "Martha girls" often saw action as nurses to the wounded. Martha Washington College consolidated with Emory and Henry in 1919 but in 1932 closed its doors. The facility reopened three years later as an inn.

Martha Washington is furnished with legions of antiques beyond description, many of which were brought out of basement retirement during the renovation. Richly colored carpet, ornate antique beds, elaborate window treatments and interiors dressed to the nines greet you everywhere. Intriguing, colorful murals portraying periods of history adorn the hallway entrance. The veranda provides a delightful place to relax in antique rocking chairs.

Guest rooms invoke more superlative descriptions. The suites have ice makers, phones in the bathrooms, specialty soaps, shampoos, monogrammed robes for your traveling convenience, and a jacuzzi in many of the baths. For $250 you can reserve the Governor's Suite.

The luxurious accommodations will make you wish for a longer stay. Fine service is the rule here and more than compares with the sophistication of the nation's top rated stars.

The cuisine is excellent, with a menu that changes several times a year. Victorian in design, the First Lady's Table dining room features a wide selection of continental and old southern fare. Fresh flowers top the tables. Breakfast, lunch and dinner cost separately from your lodging. Tea time is a 4 to 5 p.m. ritual.

Room service is available if you want to dine in your private quarters. Civil War memorabilia line the walls of the Pub, where there is dancing to live entertainment nightly. Act II, a more casual lounge, also has a dance floor, in addition to the romance of a fireplace and Barter Theatre trivia wall hangings.

The Grand Ballroom holds 300 and is well suited for multiple purposes from conventions to receptions. The silk moire wallpaper, sculptured satin draperies and marbleized woodwork play up the room's splendor. The East Parlor, polished with original oil paintings and antiques, accommodates smaller parties well. The Board Room offers another formal area for meetings.

Small Pleasures Gift Shop carries such items from around the world as Fitz and Floyd china, Gordon Frazier wrapping paper, wines and Thistle pottery. Locally crafted goods range from prints to jellies.

Martha Washington Inn offers several promotional weekends. "Escape to the Martha" is a weekend deal that includes some meals. The "Fall Foliage Escapade" fills up fast. Virginia's mountains flame too brilliantly for many travelers to pass up. "Magic at the Martha" is exclusive to honeymooners. And the "Thanksgiving Harvest" is a good holiday option.

Don't leave this genteel place without inquiring about the mysterious violin player on the third floor or the riderless horse sometimes seen on the front lawn. You may or may not want to know about the blood stain that could not be removed from the front of one room and was thus hidden by carpet.

From the Martha Washington Inn you will definitely want to walk across the street to attend a play at the world-

famous Barter Theatre. Founded during the Depression when food was bartered for tickets, the theater holds the record for being America's longest running professional equity theater.

Dixie Pottery sells an enormous range of gifts from around the world. White's Mill, a Virginia landmark, will interest you with its old timey operation. You can purchase some freshly ground meal or fish the trout pond. The Cave House Craft Shop three blocks from the inn sells local folk art. There are numerous other shops filled with antiques and collectibles. Abingdon is one

of those history havens with a walking tour designed to show off its tree-lined streets, brick sidewalks and picturesque homes.

Hiking the nearby Appalachian Trail across Virginia's highest peak and biking the country roads are other favorite pastimes. The Virginia Creeper trail begins one mile from the inn. ♫

*150 West Main St.*
*Abingdon, VA 24210*
*In Virginia: 800/553-1014*
*Elsewhere: 703/628-3161*
*Exit 8, I-81, into Abingdon.*

# FOUR & TWENTY BLACKBIRDS

*Sing a Song of Sixpence*

This small, overnight inn lies in the heart of Virginia's hunt country, just an hour's drive from Washington, D.C., or Charlottesville. It's ten miles east of historic Washington, Virginia, and ten miles west of Warrenton.

The restored farmhouse, situated on 150 acres, was built in the 1860s. There are three guest rooms, air-conditioned and comfortably furnished with wonderful antiques and collectibles.

Innkeepers Vincent Deluise and Heide Morf enjoy serving their guests. Food is their first love. At the breakfast table you'll find fresh-squeezed juice and homemade muffins along with your pancakes, omelet or waffles. Your innkeepers also offer an optional dinner menu that explores a wide range of ethnic and American regional cuisines with artistry and unpretentious elegance. Pastas, breads, ice creams and even the after-dinner mints are all homemade. The vegetables are picked fresh from the garden. The wine list includes well chosen selections from several area vineyards.

Before they became innkeepers, Vinnie and Heidi worked at several area restaurants, including a five-star, internationally recognized one.

Behind their inn is a small gift shop affectionately named "One Man's Trash." It's guaranteed to offer some fascinating old treasures that you can't possibly live without.

Four and Twenty Blackbirds is surrounded by wildflower meadows at the eastern edge of beautiful Rappahannock County. Photography enthusiasts, amateur and professional alike, ought to schedule an early May visit to capture some of nature's prize moments. The fields beside the house are covered with wild red poppies.

Your easy-going hosts will tell you where to find their favorite antique shops. They can give you directions to some good hiking trails, or point you to the good angles on birdwatching. Feeding the donkeys, midnight star-gazing, or an afternoon stroll picking a pocketfull of rye are among the simple pleasures to be had here. You are also close to the Skyline Drive, Luray Caverns, wineries, the Bealeton Flying Circus, and weekend plays or movies at the Gay Street Theater. Your hosts are happy to help you plan an outing. Old Rag Mountain is a favorite hiking destination, the Thornton River a favorite of canoeists.

If your idea of a weekend getaway is doing almost nothing, Heidi and Vinnie invite you to sit around the flower gardens with a good book, play a slow game of boccie ball across the lawn, or just put your feet up on the front porch and watch the corn grow. Four and Twenty Blackbirds is a special country inn with wonderful food and a friendly, relaxed atmosphere. Your first visit here won't be your last.

*P.O. Box 95*
*Amissville, VA 22002*
*703/937-5885*

*Between Warrenton and Washington, Va., on Rt. 211. Reservations confirmed with payment of one night's lodging. Full refund if cancelled 72 hours prior to check-in.*

# MEMORY HOUSE
*Vintage Victorian*

If you want to escape the hustle-bustle of highrise lodging in Washington, D.C., but you still need to be close to the nation's capital, head for Memory House. Access is easy because it's just off Interstate 66 on Washington Boulevard in Arlington, Virginia. You will surely enjoy the old-fashioned comfort and friendship.

John and Marlys McGrath bought the house in 1977. They named it Memory House because of its happy heritage down through the years. The colorful, frame building is located on a spacious corner lot in what used to be a cornfield in East Falls Church. Harry and Alice Murray Fellows had the home built in 1899. And, if guests today close their eyes a moment, they can visualize what it was like in the early days when only a dirt lane led up to the home.

The McGraths, with incredible attention to detail, have been faithfully re-storing the home to its former state. From a 1904 photograph they had an identical, cast iron tower cresting made and mounted on the exterior where one had stood. The gingerbread was restored to its original detail and the house painted in warm, Victorian colors. Your hosts added a butterfly weathervane of stained glass, their own touch to enhance the color scheme.

Inside is no less a work of art: colorful stenciling, reproduction pressed-tin ceilings, refinished period antiques, prize-winning needlepoint handworked by John, an etched glass powder room door from Washington's old Dodge Hotel, a bathroom as Victorian as they come and a treasure trove of "trash," now turned into opulent objets d' art.

The tender affection with which the innkeepers have restored their home is evident. It shows up in the gardens, architecture, furniture refinishing, interior design and Victorian crafts. The B&B has two rooms, one with a half bath and one with a shared bath. Breakfast is included in your room rate.

You can walk a block to the subway (East Falls Church Station) and 15 minutes later be at the Mall in Washington. I-66 will take you there by car in 10 minutes.

Memory House is in a neighborhood with a park, equipped with picnic tables and tennis courts. You are in walking distance of a basketball court and bike trail system. Shops and restaurants are within eight blocks. And, of course, if you have come to sightsee, there is all of Washington with its unlimited things to do and see.

*6404 N. Washington Blvd.*
*Arlington, VA 22205*
*703/534-4607*

*Exit 22 from I-66, onto Washington Blvd.*

Unbeknownst to many seasoned travelers, Virginia does have a sliver of real estate between the Chesapeake Bay and the Atlantic Ocean. It's called the Eastern Shore.

As you might suspect, there are not many towns along this strip of land. Cape Charles is among the ever so few. But Amanda's Bed and Breakfast Reservation Service offers accommodations on this remote tip of Virginia.

You come here for the unspoiled land, abundant wildlife, game birds, and nature's most fabulous sunsets and sunrises. You come here to get away from the rat race. You come here to enjoy memorable breakfasts.

The lovely homes on Amanda's listing feature private beaches, tasteful interiors furnished with antiques and country crafts, and comfortable amenities. The prevalent architectural styles are Victorian and Colonial. Amanda's B&B at Cape Charles is within walking distance to the only public beach fronting on the Chesapeake Bay.

You pass the time away here in low gear — strolling down a mile-long promenade, sitting on a porch where you can sniff the salty air and watch the sun disappear in glorious array behind the blue-green water, enjoying nature and just plain relaxing.

There is something very satisfying about walking down secluded country roads, under tall pines and oaks. Feasting on soft shell crab sandwiches and fresh fish at the quaint eateries is worth the visit alone. Truck farming has kept generations of families on the shore, so it's a tightly-knit but friendly community.

Fishing boats are available for charter. The bay is the largest estuary in the United States and abounds with unlimited delights. The swimming is excellent. Nearby are historic sights, the Nature Conservancy and the U.S. Fish and Wildlife Refuge. Your hosts grew up in the area and have a storehouse of local knowledge.

As unto itself as it is, the Eastern Shore is easily accessible from Baltimore, Washington, Richmond or Charlottesville. Cape Charles is a pleasant morning or early evening drive from these metropolises. The Bay Bridge Tunnel, a real treat for children and adults, connects the Virginia Beach area to the southern end of the Eastern Shore. A quiet, peaceful B&B awaits you at the end of the trail.

Amanda's, representing private B&B owners elsewhere on the Eastern Shore and in six states, can arrange one night or an entire trip for you. Going north from Cape Charles, Amanda's has a unique Victorian B&B in Arlington. This Victorian-style home is decorated to the nines and is also easily convenient to National Airport.

Other homes on the registry include many on the National Historic Registry, as well as some unusual homes in very special neighborhoods. They all have style, charm and facilities to meet your needs. Some have pools, jacuzzies, fireplaces, private decks and picturesque gardens. The accommodations are perfect for newlyweds. Available as a practical solution to your gift-buying problems, gift certificates for the B&B's transcend all occasions and ages.

*Amanda's Bed and Breakfast*
*Reservation Service*
*1428 Park Ave.*
*Baltimore, MD 21217*
*301/225-0001*

*Reservation secured by night's deposit.*
*Refunds if cancelled 1 week prior to arrival, minus $25 service fee.*

*The Eastern Shore, along the Chesapeake Bay, America's largest estuary.*

# EDGEWOOD PLANTATION
*A   James   River   Manor*

Some of the jewels of Virginia's past are the surviving plantation homes that front the James River. The Jamestown settlement eventually pushed into Williamsburg in the early founding days, and from there growing prosperity edged up along the James because the river afforded a good transportation link for colonists moving tobacco and the other cash crops to overseas markets.

Books have been written about these famous homes that enshrine so much of America's early history. Some are open to the public for touring and some are privately owned. Edgewood Plantation is one you can sleep in! Once a part of Berkeley Plantation, this B&B includes

a mill and a home that are both National and State Historical Landmarks.

In view from Route 5, the Carpenters' Gothic house was built in 1849 by northerner Spencer Rowland, 30 years before the style was popular in the south. It has been used as a Civil War lookout tower, restaurant, church, post office, telephone exchange and nursing home, with a history closely tied to the life of the community.

The profile of guests is legendary. Gen. Jeb Stuart of the Confederate Army stopped at Edgewood for coffee, on his way to Richmond to warn Gen. Robert E. Lee of the Union strength.

Stories of unrequited love abound, too. Lizzie Rowland, whose name is

etched in her upstairs bedroom window, died of a broken heart after waiting in vain for her lover to return from the Civil War. The prevailing belief is that she still waits at the upstairs front window for him to come from nearby Shirley Plantation. With all its history and romance, Edgewood embodies an intimate, home atmosphere.

A 1725 mill and mill race, erected by Benjamin Harrison, lies several yards from the house. The mill was unusual in that the wheel was positioned inside, instead of on the outside. At one time the mill used to grind the corn for all the nearby farms. You will appreciate the serenity of the grounds created by a gazebo.

Edgewood encompasses 14 large rooms, 10 fireplaces, five tall chimneys and a freestanding, winding, three-story staircase. The hostess, dressed in Victorian garb, will give you a guided tour. Six unique and elegant rooms are available for overnight guests. Each comes with its own sitting area and a particular decor. The honeymoon suite and Victorian, Civil War, Rebecca's, Scarlett's and Sarah's rooms are loaded with antiques and popular English country pieces. You soon realize you've entered a collector's haven and will discover a shopping treat at the gift shop. The abundant antique clothing and linens throughout the house especially give you a feel for the lifestyle of the old era.

In contrast to the multitude of antiques and old-fashioned country artifacts, a modern hot tub and swimming pool are provided for the pleasure of guests. They are a soothing place to relax after a day of touring the other James River plantations. You will also want to take in the sights of Williamsburg, Petersburg, Surry County, Hopewell and Richmond.

Guests are served complimentary refreshments after arrival and a full country breakfast in the morning by candlelight in the formal dining room or in the intriguing country kitchen. Edgewood caters wedding receptions, luncheons and teas. Its popularity peaks at Christmas, amid festive decorations and holiday activity, an old-timey sleigh, 15 decorated trees and hot mulled cider, so make your Christmas reservations well in advance.

Charles City *is* "Old Virginia," a place where time seems to have been put on hold. Your friendly hosts, Julian and Dot Boulware, send out a warm welcome. And one thing for certain — they display one of the best collections of memorabilia of any B&B in the Commonwealth of Virginia. **⌇**

*Rt. 2, Box 490*
*Charles City, VA 23030*
*804/829-2962*

*On Rt. 5 in Charles City County.*
*Halfway between Washington and Richmond, 1/4 mile from Berkeley, 3 miles from Shirley and 2 miles from Evelynton Plantation.*

# CHESTER
*Constitution Route*

Charlottesville/Scottsville

In 1847 Joseph C. Wright, a retired landscape architect from Chester, England, built a Greek Revival estate that today greets the bed and breakfast fancier in spectacular splendor.

History oozes from this haven on the James River, punctuated with historical homesteads all along its curvey path to the Chesapeake Bay. Chester is on the outskirts of Charlottesville and is just off Route 20, called the Constitution Route because it links so many Revolutionary War memories between Fredericksburg and Appomattox.

Major James Hill, the local Confederate Army commander, head-

quartered at Chester. During the last month of the Civil War, Union troops destroyed parts of Scottsville. General Sheridan and his aide, Colonel George Custer (later of Custer's Last Stand fame) went to arrest Major Hill but left him alone because they thought he was going to die from his battle wounds. Hill, however, survived!

Not only does history peek around the corner at you, but the carefully landscaped lawns of old spill over with Garden Week beauty. More than 30 varieties of trees and shrubs, enormous stands of English boxwood lining the walks, a towering white pine tree and perhaps the largest holly tree in Al-

bemarle County cover seven lush acres. From time to time the grounds have been opened for Garden Week.

The unusual layout of this stately manse yields five large guest rooms, four with fireplaces. The expansive living, dining and library/music rooms also have fireplaces. You are privy to three relaxing porches. And you'll find wood in your room to feed a cozy fire.

The hosts, world travelers who retired from the New York business world, insure a convivial stay for their guests. Artifacts from their global jaunts, antiques and oriental carpets fill the columned mansion. Because the hosts breed and show Russian wolfhounds, they also offer excellent facilities for visiting pets.

All rooms are nicely appointed and tastefully decorated. One guest room connects with a sitting room. The neatly trimmed room sports a queensized, four-poster bed, a pedestal sink and semi-private bath. A three-quarter, four-poster, antique spool bed graces the downstairs bedroom — the one guest quarters with private bath.

The full English breakfast meets hunger with juice, fresh melon in season, bacon, sausage, eggs to order, pancakes, homemade vegetable breads, waffles, coffee and tea. Tea and biscuits are available at tea time. You can snack on fruit, canapes, soft drinks and beer. With advance reservations you can dine in elegance on a four-course, Continental dinner served with wine.

Innkeepers Gordon Anderson and Dick Shaffer like to socialize, so you're liable to find a party-like atmosphere almost nightly.

You will not run out of things to do. You can enjoy satellite television in the library, bicycle (supplied by hosts) around historic Scottsville, attend summer concerts at Ash Lawn, or experience the nation's last, old-style poled ferry across the James. Outdoor buffs can fish, tube or canoe the James and swim Lake Reynovia. Sightseers can visit the homes of presidents Thomas Jefferson and James Monroe, Michie Tavern, Charlottesville and University of Virginia, the Skyline Drive or Blue Ridge Parkway. One new "must" is Montpelier, James and Dolley Madison's home, which was closed to the public until 1987.

James T. Yenckel, Washington Post travel writer, summed up Chester's congeniality when he said in a review, "We felt so much like invited house guests...."

*Rt. 4, Box 57*
*Scottsville, VA 24590*
*804/286-3960*

*From Charlottesville I-64/Exit 24, take Rt. 20 south for 17 miles, right onto Rt. 726, 2 1/2 blocks. From Richmond take Rt. 6 west to Scottsville, left on 726. 25% deposit with reservation: fully refundable with 10 days' cancellation notice.*

# CLIFTON
*A Jefferson Property*

A few miles east of Charlottesville, on 10 acres of secluded woodland overlooking the Rivanna River and the foothills to the Blue Ridge Mountains, lies Clifton: The Country Inn. Originally part of the Jefferson family estate Shadwell, the property was given by Thomas Jefferson to his eldest daughter Martha when she married Thomas Mann Randolph, who went on to become a Virginia governor.

Clifton derives its name from the fact that it sits upon a cliff. Begun in 1799, it was one of the early large plantation properties in Albemarle County and is flanked by Jefferson's Monticello,

Monroe's Ash Lawn, Michie's Tavern, and the University of Virginia. This is awesome territory! History everywhere.

On the grounds of Clifton are a brick cottage, which served as the law office of Thomas Randolph; a carriage house, restored with architectural salvage (including bath fixtures) from the recently demolished Meriwether Lewis House; and the main house, a classic plantation manor home. A long driveway makes a U-curve in front of the country inn. Very tranquil.

Your hosts are as genuine and friendly as they come. They will make you feel right at home in their historic abode.

The tasteful accommodations and refined food dictate that you will also come back!

A luxurious escape, the 18th century manor house retains much of its original appearance and feel. The same pine floors, paneled walls and fireplaces (there is one in every room) that warmed Jefferson's family on visits will welcome you. Clifton and its history have not been manufactured or restored — they have been cherished and maintained.

The sleeping quarters are large, private and comfortable. Four of the seven rooms have suite configurations.

Each room has a private bath and its own woodburning fireplace. Beds are queen-sized four-poster or canopied. They are made up with crisp, line-dried, 100 percent cotton sheets, and luxurious down comforters. Bath towels are lush cotton terries.

Your tariff includes breakfast: fresh muffins with pecans, black raspberry streusel, apple-walnut-raisin muffins, fresh fruit compote, juices, Belgian waffles, three-cheese omelet and garden vegetable quiche. Upon arrival, you are offered some light refreshment. The sizable back terrace is available for dining and peaceful relaxation.

If you can make your way from the delectable spread, some beautiful grounds outside await you. Flower-lined, stone walkways lead to the other buildings. Mini walking trails throughout the wooded property provide you much natural enjoyment.

Other than the gentle baaing of Clifton's sheep or lowing of the neighbor's cattle, civilization noises are left in nearby Charlottesville. There are woods for you to explore, a private lake to fish or swim in, gardens to browse, clay courts to play tennis on, manicured lawns for croqueting and a pool to swim some laps in. When the leaves are off the trees, you can see Monticello on the neighboring hill. If you let your imagination stir, you can see Jefferson strolling his grounds.

Nearby points of interest include Jefferson's Monticello, Michie Tavern, the University of Virginia, wineries, historic Charlottesville, the Skyline Drive and Blue Ridge Parkway. If you really want to enjoy the outdoors you have the option of a good horseback ride near Clifton. ▟

*Rt. 9, Box 412*
*Charlottesville, VA 22901*
*804/971-1800*

*Just off Rt. 250 east, on Rt. 729 in Shad-*
*well. Full refund of deposit up to 10*
*days prior to reservation.*

# NICHOLA
*Log Cabin Intimacy*

If you have always wanted to live in your very own log cabin, you will at least get a chance to sample such life here. The authentic, 200-year-old log dwelling sits on 150 acres of farmland owned by a physician and his family. The cabin overlooks spectacular views of the Blue Ridge Mountains.

You are only 10 minutes from the Blue Ridge Parkway and Appalachian Trail. The Parkway extends 469 miles along the crest of the Southern Appalachians and links two eastern national parks — Shenandoah and Great Smoky Mountains. It begins nearby at Afton Mountain. A visitor center at Humpback Rocks can give you the information you need for enjoying America's most popular parkway this side of California. There is no fee for traveling the Parkway, which scientists claim has more varieties of flora and fauna than any place in the world.

The beloved Appalachian Trail, which traverses the states from Maine to Georgia, zigzags through Virginia and follows the Parkway for a while. The trail is well-marked and kept in good condition.

So if you're an outdoors person, you'll find the cabin a fitting launching pad. Its romantic setting will also appeal to couples. Honeymooners are served champagne! Breakfast is delivered in a picnic basket, brimming with fresh fruit, homemade muffins, fresh coffee or tea, and juice. Your innkeeper's specialties are sour cream muffins and Furnace Creek date bread. In good weather, you may want to spread out your breakfast on the outdoor picnic table.

A basket of fresh fruit greets you at your arrival. Your breakfast is also included in the cabin rate. For your other meals you are minutes away from a very nice restaurant in Ivy. Within six to seven minutes you can reach additional good eating places.

Inside the cabin, a large central room heated with a wood stove and a small bath are furnished comfortably.

You are free to visit with the farm animals, roam the countryside or play tennis on the family courts.

Because of the natural surroundings, the cabin is very popular during the fall and spring months. You will want to make reservations well in advance for those times. Nichola is one of those rare B&B's suited for young children, incidentally. Innkeepers provide a crib and playpen. 🍴

*Guesthouses*
*P. O. Box 5737*
*Charlottesville, VA 22905*
*804/979-7264*

*Phone reservation between 12-5 p. m., weekdays.*
*With 7 days' notice, deposit returned minus $15 service charge.*

# OLD SLAVE QUARTERS
*An Upstairs Suite*

The exterior of this unique cottage will charm even the most sophisticated. Its cozy feeling gives you an immediate invitation to come right on in. But not before you fall in love with the immense boxwoods and the cascading terraced garden bordered with wooden benches.

Surrounded by lovely gardens of wildflowers, the Old Slave Quarters has a small pond and the foundations of an old ice house on its premises. The B&B lies in the heart of a neighborhood graced with grand old homes.

It is a fascinating place to stay. Old Slave Quarters was originally constructed as a tenant dwelling on a 480-acre farm owned by John Kelly. Thomas Jefferson once tried to buy it for the University of Virginia's Rotunda, but Kelly, an ardent Federalist, refused vehemently. Later, the structure served as a kitchen and quarters for the Preston house built in the 1850s.

The current owners have furnished the home with a harmonious mixture of very old antiques and contemporary art. Enhancing the interesting decor are American, English and Oriental antiques and art objects. A rare set of Windsor chairs made in Kentucky around 1820 are the focal point of the dining room.

You have the privacy of your own entrance to the upstairs suite. The guest area consists of a sitting room, a bedroom with a king-sized bed and another bedroom with a single bed. There is one bath with a tub, sans shower.

In the sitting room you can open a couch for a double bed to accommodate additional family members, so the quarters can comfortably sleep five.

Especially convenient for University of Virginia guests, Slave Quarters is adjacent to UVA and fraternity row. Nearby are many riding stables, three presidential homes, the Blue Ridge Mountains and other natural wonders. You have opportunities for tubing, canoeing or fishing on the James River,

ballooning and hiking.

The Old Slave Quarters, owned by Guesthouses proprietor Mary Hill Caperton, is but one of more than 60 accommodations offered by her Guesthouses B&B Reservation Service in Charlottesville and Albemarle County. Established in 1976, Guesthouses was the first bed and breakfast reservation service in the United States! It is also the largest in Virginia. In true southern fashion, it has set the pace for gracious hospitality.

Included in the listings are historic estates. To serve the bed and breakfast traveler well, Guesthouses categorizes its establishments according to deluxe, quality, comfort or estate cottages.

All are in prestigious town or country locations in the proximity of Monticello, the University of Virginia and the Blue Ridge. The Charlottesville area is where I-64, U.S. 29 and U.S. 250 all come together in the center of the state.

Guesthouses also offers several B&B's in Luray, an hour and a half northwest of Charlottesville. Your hosts try to match your personal needs and tastes with just the right place. Break-

fast is included in all the rates and might range from self-serve continental to home-cooked gourmet. A $4 surcharge is added to one-night stays.

Deluxe cottage and leisure homes range from $80 to $150 per night. With various stages in between, Guesthouses offers budget B&B's starting at $48 per couple per night. Weekly and monthly rates are also available.

Charlottesville is 347 miles from New York City, 161 from Baltimore, 120 from D.C., 70 from Richmond, 121 from Williamsburg, 259 from Philadelphia, 581 from Boston and 512 from Atlanta. ▯

*Guesthouses*
*P.O. Box 5737*
*Charlottesville, VA 22905*
*804/979-8327*

*Reservation hours from 12-5, Mon.-Fri. 25% deposit. Cancellations with 7 days' notice; deposit returned minus $15 service fee.*

# HIGH MEADOWS
*Renaissance in the Vineyard*

There are restorations and there are restorations. But innkeepers Peter and M. Jae Abbitt Sushka "redid" their Federalist-Victorian home in such exacting detail that it qualified as a Virginia Historic Landmark and a National Historic Home.

The energetic, creative couple, like others around the Commonwealth, were smitten with the bed and breakfast bug while living in England. Peter, now retired, was serving as a submarine commander for the U. S. Navy. Jae was completing her M. B. A. The old world, country inn tradition captivated them, so they started plotting a plan to find a quality location in the states where

weary travelers could forget the "day-to-day busyness" of life.

Peter and Jae purchased High Meadows, outside of Charlottesville, in 1985. They commuted from their weekday jobs in Washington, D. C., in the initial months of turning their finely disguised gem from a leaky hulk with no electricity or plumbing into a more than habitable country inn. They did much of the work themselves and only subcontracted when necessary.

The Sushkas openly admit "the restoration process was a struggle in the organization and stretching of time, money and energy." Today they relish sharing their experiences and restora-

tion tales, many of which reveal the amusing side of human nature. Despite all the plaster dust, bruised bodies, late hours of planning, endless paperwork and inflexible building codes, the innkeepers never wavered from their goal: to provide "a pleasant respite for our guests to relive history, a retreat into a special moment before assaulting life's mainstream again and a haven of the past, when, although life was difficult, it had a slower civility."

Known as Fairview until 1920, High Meadows now consists of seven guest rooms, five with private bath and one with whirlpool. The spacious rooms are furnished with period antiques. Altogether, the home has 17 rooms and nine fireplaces. One outstanding feature is the original grained woodwork.

The first part of the estate was built in 1832 on 44 acres. A "2-over-2" brick structure, the home of merchant Peter White had six rooms. In 1882 Charles Harris, who bought the land, added a stuccoed home on the property. Around 1890 the prosperous businessman connected his Victorian home to the earlier Federal building via a covered hall. Today there is no other structure in Virginia like High Meadows.

The restoration of the two guest rooms in the Federalist portion was patterned after the simplicity of Gunston Hall, George Mason's 18th century northern Virginia estate. The Victorian house is embellished with the lavish feel of the late 19th century.

Jae's associate degree in horticulture and Peter's experience and creativity equipped the couple to professionally landscape the inn's 22 acres. Her antique rose garden is unique, and she provides a comprehensive listing that will thrill any rosarian. Guests will also enjoy touring the other flower gardens or wandering through the vineyard of pinot noir grapevines. The grounds are ideal for picnicking and birdwatching.

Footpaths lead to a couple of ponds and trickling creeks. A romantic memory of a bygone era, the gazebo affords you a private retreat amid dogwood, hollies and yellow Scotch broom. For lounging you can take your pick among four porches. The more ambitious can take a bicycle ride; play croquet, badminton, or horseshoes; or tour the surrounding area.

You are staying on the Constitution Highway, so named for the framers of the Constitution who lived and traveled on this beautiful, dogwood-lined road. The presidential homes of Jefferson, Monroe and Madison are open to the public. Local wineries offer tours and tasting. The town of Scottsville is so historic it is also on the National Register. There are antique shops and museums, and canoeing, tubing and fishing on the James River. Perhaps one of the most special times of the year is fall foliage, from mid-September to early November. The Blue Ridge Mountains arise from the Piedmont region here.

Wintergreen, at the top of the ridge, offers good skiing during the winter.

During your stay at High Meadows you get a four-course breakfast: fresh fruit, homemade breads and muffins, gourmet egg dishes, and coffee or tea. In the evening you are offered Virginia wines for tasting and hors d'oeuvres. On weekends the inn offers dinner by candlelight and, on request any evening, gourmet picnics are available. The innkeepers, both schooled in international cooking classes, have been asked so often for their recipes that they plan to publish a cookbook. ◢

Route 4, Box 6
Scottsville, VA 24590
804/286-2218

Exit 24 off I-64. Follow Rt. 20 for 17.6 miles, turn left at inn's sign.
$25 to confirm reservations; all but $10 refundable within 2 weeks of booking.

# PROSPECT HILL

*Two Centuries Away*

A boxwood hedge along the entrance way signals you are approaching Prospect Hill, a 1732 plantation in a little out-of-the-way place called Trevilians. Here, not far from Charlottesville, are rare magnolias, tall tulip poplars, giant beeches — a graceful English tree garden shading the manor house. A few paces away rest the slave quarters, the overseer's house, slave kitchen, smoke house and carriage house.

You might pause to watch a squirrel scampering across the open lawn, which rolls on for a quarter of a mile into the Virginia countryside. Tantalizing smells from the kitchen will draw you inside, but not before you enjoy another deep breath of the sweet, clear country air.

Not much has changed here in the last two centuries. In 1732 the Roger Thompson family converted an existing barn into a house after the log cabin dwelling became too small. Richmond Terrill purchased the small farm in 1793 and added additional slave quarters. The property passed into the hands of William Overton in 1840, and he gradually enlarged the land holdings to 1,576 acres. He built two wings onto the home and put in a spiral staircase.

After the War Between the States, the Overtons' son returned to find his family plantation overgrown and his slaves gone. To make ends meet, he did what many other southern families were forced to do — take in guests from the city. In 1880 he built on some more

bedrooms and also expanded the old slave quarters to accommodate guests.

For over a century now Prospect Hill has established a tradition of hospitality. Your innkeepers today, Mirelle and Bill Sheehan, along with their children Mike and Nancy, lay out an informal welcome mat. Their comfortable and relaxing style will put you at ease. So will the modern whirlpool baths in some of the guest rooms.

For shelter you can choose the restored slave quarters, with their beamed ceiling, squeaky floors and crackling fireplaces, or opt for the rooms in the manor house, with their antique furnishings and exquisite quilts. Most of these guest rooms also have fireplaces. A private veranda overlooks the hillside.

There are 11 rooms in all at the manor house and its dependencies, which are newly decorated and have modern bathrooms, some with jacuzzies.

You begin your day with a full country breakfast, as you desire — in bed or at a table in your room. You will know dinner time by the ring of the bell. As is the age-old tradition, the innkeeper serves you what he has prepared for his family. The four to five course meal is served in three candlelit dining rooms and is preceded by the blessing, followed by leisurely dining and cheerful fellowship. The menu usually consists of basic dishes with French Provencale accents. Country fare at its best! Dinner, by the way, is served to the public for $25, Wednesday through Saturday only. The innkeepers can cater to special diets if you request such during reservations.

Tea time is also part of the ritual at Prospect Hill. You may enjoy a glass of sherry before dinner, out on the grounds or in front of the fireplace inside. Seasoned travelers have been heard to declare that Prospect Hill is one of the nicest B&B's you'll find anywhere.

The rambling yellow inn is situated in the Green Springs Historic District of Louisa County. For this reason you may find that the greatest pleasure of all is "back roading" it. The area is also good for antiquing, hunting, biking, hiking, swimming, or visiting Monticello, Ashlawn, University of Virginia, the Skyline Drive and Blue Ridge Parkway.

Court Square has neat gift items in Charlottesville. Montpelier, the home of President James Madison and his wife Dolley, opened by the National Trust for public tours in 1987, is a short ride away in Montpelier. The Barboursville Vineyards, also nearby in Orange County, was the first Virginia winery to grow *vitis vinifera* in the Commonwealth, reviving Jefferson's dream. The Oakencroft Vineyard and Winery, another of Virginia's most celebrated farm wineries, is just west of Charlottesville's city limits.

*Rt. 3, Box 430*
*Trevilians, VA 23093*
*703/967-0844*
*From Richmond 50 miles: I-64 to Exit 27, Rt. 15 south to Zion Crossroads. Left on Rt. 250 east. One mile to Rt. 613, turn left. Go 3 miles, Prospect Hill on left. Closed Christmas Eve and Day. One night's lodging deposit required. Refunded, less $5, with 10 - day notice. Best time for reservations, 9 a.m - 5 p.m..*

# SILVER THATCH INN

*Worlds Apart*

Professionally trained in the culinary and hostelry arts, Tim and Shelley Dwight have transformed a 200-year-old Hessian log barracks — one of the oldest buildings in Central Virginia — into a premier colonial inn. You leave the computerized, mechanized 20th century behind once you stroll up the flower-lined, brick walk straightway to the entrance. You quickly settle into the old world charm and savor every relaxing moment of it.

Comfortable country elegance at its best. Exciting interiors filled with antiques, native folk art and cozy corners. Richly decorated walls drenched in deep chocolates, maroons and greens. Hand-painted wood trim. Canopy drapes of imported fabrics. Little courtyards where in pleasant weather you can sip from a wine list extraordinaire (Tim's cellar of over 200

vintage wines has earned Silver Thatch *Wine Spectator's* award for having one of the outstanding wine lists in the world). Magnificent elms and dogwood, the state's tree, visible everywhere. Panoramic views of rolling green fields that give way to the beautiful Blue Ridge Mountains. Candlelight dining in the finest sense.

Built on the site of an Indian village, the inn has seen life as a Revolutionary War prisoner camp, boys' school, tobacco plantation, melon farm, home to a University of Virginia (UVA) dean, Hollymead Restaurant, and since 1984 when the Dwights bought it, the Silver Thatch Inn.

Tim, maitre d' and sommelier for the restaurant, is owner-operator of the full-service country inn. His wife Shelley is chef de cuisine. Inspired by variety themselves, they change their superior country French menu each month. The

fare often boasts local veal, out-of-the-ordinary seafood, duck, unusual desserts and Virginia wines.

The guest rooms and furnishings are as elegant as the food. The Dwights, who did the extensive renovations themselves, have kept intact the unique style of their colonial habitat, which has seven overnight rooms, four with fireplaces; three dining rooms; and sunroom and lounge.

The Hessian Room is in the two-story, white frame cabin built by Hessian soldiers in 1789 after they were taken prisoner at the battle of Saratoga and brought down from New York. The English Room, occupying the 1812 wing of the house, once served as the boys' school but now is a dining area. The 1937 wing originally added by the UVA dean for his library, serves as the Hollymead Room and lounge. These three adjoining structures form the main inn.

Three of the guest rooms are located here. In a separate little cottage are four bedrooms. Snatches of antique clothing hang here and there or framed on walls.

Interesting architectural details highlight the Washington Room: pine slats over the bed are set into dry wall and edged in green.

To enter the Thomas Jefferson Room on the upper floor you almost have to duck through the low door opening. A crocheted top and triangular patch quilt adorn that canopy bed, alongside an antique carriage seat.

The Madison Room also has a four-poster bed covered by a colorful patchwork quilt. You view the courtyard from the room's five windows. Blue and red stenciling; country print sheets; a restored, flat-top, wooden trunk; and a Williamsburg-red mantel warm the room.

Lovely amenities abound in the bathrooms: lingerie sachet, special shampoos and soaps, English mending kit, night light and stained glass.

The inn is filled with fresh flowers and plants, dried arrangements, hanging baskets. Heart-shaped chocolates wrapped in red foil await you in your room with a bottle of wine.

Well suited for couples, the inn is also ideal for gatherings of up to 20 people. Because they enjoy the colonial romance of the retreat in the hills, the personalized attention, the haute cuisine, and the well-appointed rooms, guests have been beating a path back for repeat visits. The Dwights maintain a mailing list for their loyal clientele.

Silver Thatch puts you in the middle of Mr. Jefferson's historic country and minutes away from UVA, Monticello, Michie Tavern and James Monroe's Ash Lawn. Afton Mountain, where the Skyline Drive goes north and the Blue Ridge Parkway heads south, is 20 minutes west, near Wintergreen, which offers skiing. You can ramble the back roads of colonial America, enjoy fox hunting and steeplechases, tour wineries, or search for antiques. When all that's exhausted, you can collapse into a backgammon game at the inn's firelit pub. ▌

*3001 Hollymead Rd.*
*Charlottesville, VA 22901*
*804/978-4686*

*South of D.C., 2 hrs.; west of Richmond, 1 hr.; from Cape May, N.J., or Asheville, N.C., 7 hrs. Off Rt. 29 north on spur Rt. 1520. Deposit required within seven days of making reservations. $10 charge*

*for returned deposits. Cancellations made less than 10 days in advance must be paid in full if room can't be re-rented. Check-ins 2:30-11 p.m. Check-out 11 a.m. Dinner 5:30-9 p.m., Tues.-Sat., reservations suggested. Breakfast Sun.-Sat., lodgers only.*

# 2<sup>00</sup> SOUTH STREET
*Urban Inn*

harlottesville draws swarms of visitors for sundry reasons, and 200 South Street Inn is now one of them. Two houses, joined by a common entrance and fencing actually comprise the one address. The setting is storybook-like and gives you an accurate picture of 19th-century town life, during the days when people walked most everywhere they went.

Innkeeper Steve Deupree served as his own architect in the nine-month restoration of the inn, which occupies the downtown historic district. After

extensive detail work, the tastefully restored homes welcomed the first guest in 1986.

The small home is Victorian. The larger home was built in 1856 for Thomas Jefferson Wertenbaker, the son of Thomas Jefferson's first librarian at the University of Virginia. Later in the 20th century the residence became a girls' finishing school, then a brothel and a boarding house. The neo-classical veranda was rebuilt to perfect specifications. Inside, the massive restoration embraced the solid walnut, serpentine

handrail two-stories high in the main gallery.

Eighteenth and 19th-century English and Belgian antiques are well placed throughout the inn. English chintz and gorgeous oriental rugs accent the decor. An ongoing exhibit of Virginia artists hangs in the main gallery. The inn also houses a large part of the private collection of Holsinger photographs of early Charlottesville. You will chuckle over the juxtaposition of sleeping in a century-old canopy bed one minute and the next jumping into a 1980s whirlpool bath. Private living room suites are available, if you want them.

Bookworms are free to use the library or sitting room. Business people with work to do can go upstairs to the study. If you're in the mood to relax, head for the veranda or garden terrace. With your lodging comes a continental breakfast. Memory and Company, the inn's small but sophisticated restaurant, features new American cuisine. It opens for lunch on weekdays and for dinner on weekends, other times by special arrangements.

The inn can accommodate small meetings or provide interviewing facilities.

You are blocks away from good restaurants, shops and evening entertainment. You are one mile east of the University of Virginia, a bastion of ACC athletics. The Charlottesville-Albemarle area was not only Thomas Jefferson's territory, but home base for James Madison, James Monroe, George Rogers Clark, Meriwether Lewis and William Clark.

It's also horse country and vineyards, rivers and rolling hills. Calendar highlights include Historic Garden Week, Monticello Wine Festival, steeplechasing at Foxfield and world class jumping at Keswick.

Non-scheduled pursuits range from hiking and fishing to skiing and biking. The inn is one-half mile from the Amtrak Station and several blocks from the bus station.

*200 South St.*
*Charlottesville, VA 22901*
*804/979-0200*

*I-64 to Exit 23; at second light, right on South St., one way. Or, from Rt. 29 via 250 Bypass, McIntire Rd. to South St.*

27

# BUCKHORN INN
*Down Home Eatin'*

nown for its good food and casual dining, the Buckhorn Inn has been a landmark since 1811. Only 12 miles west of Staunton, the lovely white home serves good, country meals to many more diners than just those spending the night. It also does a lot of catering for weddings and special events.

The outstanding menu features seafood dishes and a wide selection of meat entrees, including what Virginia is famous for, country ham. Family priced, the meals come with a choice of salad, homemade rolls and tea or coffee. Vegetables of the day are served family style at your table.

All of the baking is done on the premises and reminds you of what

grandma used to fix but has often gone by the wayside with today's fast-paced culture of two-wage-earner families.

Desserts will be difficult to pass up, especially the house specialty, peanut butter pie. Buckhorn serves lunch from 11 a.m. to 3 p.m. Buffets are every night of the week from 4 till 9 and on Sundays.

Traditional Shenandoah Valley cooking isn't the only enticement you'll find at Buckhorn. For 180 years the inn has been providing a place for weary travelers to rest their heads. The rambling old home, originally called Buckhorn Tavern from 1811 to 1861, was a stopover point for people traveling to the numerous hot springs and mineral waters further to the west.

Beginning in the early 1800s, city

dwellers would flee the hot summers and retreat to the springs throughout the Allegheny Mountains. Coming in the summer and leaving in the fall, travelers also flocked from the coastal areas. They rode by stagecoach, or in their own carriages.

In an 1854 letter, Stonewall Jackson's first wife wrote to her husband's sister that she had stayed here for several days enroute to the famous old Virginia springs in Bath County. This letter is part of the archives collection at the Stonewall Jackson House in Lexington.

Buckhorn itself resembles many of the homes built near the spas and springs. The stone foundation and two-story, covered, wrap-around porch are typical of the spring homes. You are standing at the gateway to spring country here, under the shade of maples and oaks.

The original tavern had eight rooms. According to the time-worn oral history, Buckhorn was known for its high-class gambling, the entertainment common to many taverns back then.

During the Civil War Battle of Mc-Dowell, many wounded soldiers were brought here. The inn was also used as quarters for officers.

Today the nicely restored inn offers comfortable lodging to the modern day traveler seeking something special and a bit of history. A two-room suite features private bath and jacuzzi. Five other rooms also have individual baths; two rooms open out to the side porch overlooking the mountain. A full country breakfast is included at no extra charge.

You are in the heart of the Shenandoah Valley and can easily take off to see and do many things. The George Washington National Forest surrounds you with its many hiking trails and scenic vistas. Fishing and hunting are superb. Other recreational sports abound.

Natural Chimneys of Mount Solon is nearby — the site of America's oldest, continuously held sporting event, the jousting tournament, which is staged each summer.

Staunton and its offerings are only minutes away, not to mention Virginia's grand dame of resorts, The Homestead, which is not quite an hour's drive to the west.

*Star Route Box 139*
*Churchville, VA 24421*
*703/337-6900*

*On Rt. 250, 12 miles west of Staunton. Not open Dec. 24-25. Restaurant closed on Monday, and during January and February also on Tuesday.*

# FOUNTAIN HALL
*For Business or Leisure*

Not much more than an hour's drive from our nation's capital, Fountain Hall is strategically positioned to serve not only small business meetings but the touring public. The inn is located in a part of Virginia where practically everything you see is historic. As even an amateur historian might suspect, George Washington surveyed the area.

Fountain Hall was originally part of a larger tract of land owned by Virginia's Royal Governor, Sir Alexander Spotswood. Built in 1859, it was named after Fountain Fisher Henry, a scion of old Virginia. Jackson Lee Fray, founder of the local phone company, bought the home in 1923 and contracted with a Philadelphia architect to build a Colonial Revival house from the

simple, country Victorian structure. The older part of the home is visible from the back. Otherwise, the average person would be hard pressed to detect that Fountain Hall ever looked any different.

Steve and Kathi Walker, and sometimes Oscar the dog, are your hosts. They can accommodate meetings and small receptions. Your hosts grew up in New York and moved from California to open Culpeper's first B&B in 1985. Steve's background is in hotel management.

Guest rooms and living areas are uniquely decorated. Rooms range from singles with shared bath to suites of two rooms with private bath and porch. Antiques abound. Your tasty breakfast will include freshly baked croissants, cheese, fruit, cereal, juice and coffee.

Giant boxwoods smartly accent Fountain Hall's front entrance. A center walkway of herringbone-patterned brick leads into cascading steps. The front entrance faces downtown Culpeper, six blocks away. From the back door you view the lazy, open space of farmland.

Points of interest are varied: Skyline Drive, Dominion Wine Cellar, Davis Street Ordinary, Montpelier (President James Madison's home that was never opened to the public until 1987), Commonwealth Horse Park and Culpeper's Historic Walking Tour.

Culpeper's history reflects a representative cross section of the history of Virginia and America. It was key in the formation of pre-Revolutionary War Virginia; two major battlefields are located at Cedar Mountain and Brandy Station. Civil War camp sites also dot the area.

If you live in a city on the Amtrak route, then Fountain Hall could be an easy target for a get-away weekend. The inn is only six short blocks from the tracks. From Chicago or Washington, D.C., you take the Cardinal line; from New Orleans, Atlanta or New York you hop on the Crescent line.

*609 South East St.*
*Culpeper, VA 22701-3222*
*703/825-6708*
*Off Rt. 29.*

*One night deposit required; refundable less 10% of total reservation amount, if two weeks' notice given. Check-in after 2 p.m.; check-out by 11 a.m.*

# BROOKFIELD
*Christmas Tree Heaven*

You are literally high up in the land of Christmas trees. Floyd County sprawls atop a long mountain plateau of the Blue Ridge. The high elevation makes it ideal for growing Christmas evergreens and that is what Brookfield Inn specializes in.

One of the largest tree farms on the East Coast, Brookfield is growing more than a half-million White Pine, Fraser Fir and Blue Spruce. This tree farm of over 800 acres was the very first grower to ship plantation fresh to the customer's door. Plantation President David Larsen even invented the UPS shipping container and he grows something for everyone, like the 6-7 foot, traditional size tree.

As you might imagine, a perfect time to head off the beaten track to the farm's modern-built inn is near Christmas. You could come home with a tree you cut yourself or a live one to plant! An old-fashioned hayride is an added incentive to come visit this rural setting. Typical of many places in Floyd, Brookfield sits a third of a mile off the public road. The boonies are everywhere up here.

As you drive along the private approach, you'll pass rhododendron, old split rail fencing, azaleas, wildflowers in profusion and a spring-fed trout pond. You may never want to leave the tranquil solitude and pure mountain air.

The bedrooms are furnished beautifully and have shared baths. Guests can roam the several acres of lawn or hike the bountiful trails. Just remember you're high in the heavens and the temperature probably is 10 degrees or more cooler than where you're from. When weather permits, guests may take their breakfast or snack on the patio.

With your room comes a southern country style breakfast of juice, coffee, baked apples, country ham, eggs or pancakes, and biscuits made by innkeeper Gaynell Thompson.

You can enjoy the Christmas spirit any time of the year, however. Santa's Workshop will teach you how to make wreaths. And several minutes away is Country Christmas House off Rt. 615. Formerly the Possum Hollow School House, the shop is open May through December, seven days a week. It carries everything you need to decorate your tree and home. Many gift items are locally crafted.

Some of the best country cooking is found in Floyd, along with some neat little shops, the real McCoy bluegrass music and an art gallery. The area is prime territory for fishing, camping, friendly mountain folks, bicycling and sightseeing gorgeous scenery. The Blue Ridge Parkway traverses the mountaintops and just down the road a piece is one of its most popular destinations, Mabry Mill.

*P.O. Box 341*
*Floyd, VA 24091*
*703/763-3363; 382-9099*
*Outside VA: 1-800-443-TREE*

*From Blue Ridge Parkway go north on Rt. 8 at Milepost 165 (Tuggles Gap), go 14 miles; the inn will be on the left.*
*From I-81, Exit 36; travel south on Rt. 8 for 12 miles.*
*Reservations needed; 48-hour cancellation policy. Check-in after 4 p.m.; check-out by 11 a.m.*

# ALDEN INN
*Greek Revival Mansion*

our chimneys in symmetrical fashion tower through the roof to clue you in that Alden is no little cabin in the woods. The eight Doric columns of the portico announce, rather dramatically, that you have arrived at a stately mansion of a bygone formal era.

With all the classic features of an imposing Greek Revival edifice, the inn is certainly impressive. The gabled rooftop is set off with an intricate balustrade. There is more perfect symmetry balancing both sides of the entrance with its windowlined doorway and overhead balcony.

Mrs. Pearl Weaver designed and built the home in 1912. In 1974, Mrs. Lucille Sanderson, the present owner, bought the place.

Inside the rooms are large. Beautiful hardwood floors peer from around the perimeters of modern-day orientals. Five bedrooms lead off from an expansive foyer upstairs, where the furnishings reflect a Victorian motif.

A parlor downstairs actually serves as an antique shop, giving guests a leisurely option for antique browsing. Period clothing is one of the shop's specialties. A living room, formal dining room and kitchen are also on this level. Guests receive a continental breakfast with their room.

Lavish wallpapers create an air of richness. Unusually striking is the dining room's oriental red wall covering with gold highlights.

Alden Inn's season runs from April 15 to November 15. The inn is located in Front Royal, the gateway to the beloved Skyline Drive, which crests the Blue Ridge Mountains (considered by some travelers to be America's most beautiful). The mountaintop roadway continues as the Blue Ridge Parkway near Waynesboro and winds south through North Carolina.

From Alden Inn you are well positioned to visit the Skyline Caverns, one of the natural wonders in Virginia's mountain region. The underground limestone deposits have made this part of the state cave country.

Guests are in walking distance of the Confederate Museum (in 1862 the battle of Front Royal opened Stonewall Jackson's famous Valley Campaign), Belle Boyd (renowned southern spy during the Civil War) Cottage, Randolph Macon Academy and a potpourri of antique, gift and craft shops.

The town of Front Royal, incorporated in 1778, derived its name from a giant oak tree that stood in the public square. In colonial days the oak was the royal tree of England.

Alden lies 70 miles west of Washington, D.C., 120 miles from Richmond and 100 miles from Baltimore. Metropolis-weary souls will find Alden a quick and easy retreat from harsh traffic.

*35 N. Royal Ave.*
*Front Royal, VA 22630*
*703/636-6645*

*I-66, from D.C.; 1-95, Rt. 17, I-66 from Richmond ; I-95, 495, 66 from Baltimore. I-66 Exit 3, left to Rt. 55. 6 miles to Rt. 340 north, 3/4 mile to Alden on right.*
*Reservations by credit cards; cancellation policy, 2 days.*

# SLEEPY HOLLOW FARM
*A Legend of Its Own*

Look for the red Sleepy Hollow mailbox, a sign that shouts "Welcome," a green barn with a very red roof, a gazebo, pond and a brick house snoozing under trees in a sleepy hollow. You have arrived at the hollow's namesake farm.

Generations of farm families have lived in the simple farmhouse. Now it attracts a wide spectrum of guests, including many international sojourners.

It remains a mystery who built the first dwelling or when, but the foundations suggests late 1700s. A two-story, three-room clapboard house was built in front of the earlier building in the 1850s. A shed kitchen was constructed later, and in 1940 two side rooms were

added and the whole house bricked over. A small, chestnut slave cabin has been renovated and a two-story addition put on. A deck leads out from the kitchen.

Two terraces, front and side porches, a croquet lawn and rooms with fireplaces promise you some low-key moments of relaxation.

Each morning you down a country breakfast in one of the main house dining rooms or on the north terrace when weather cooperates. Large glass doors render an almost ethereal view of the changing, rural landscape. The neighbor's Tarentaise bull, Angus cows and crossbred calves can be seen grazing in the fields. The formal dining

room is one of the prettiest you'll find and overlooks the herb garden and distant rolling hills. Floral accents lend outstanding splashes of color.

Sleepy Hollow is one of the few inns catering to children. A baby crib and playpen are available. The four guest rooms in the main house offer various configurations. Out back, the accommodations include two suites. Each has a bedroom with private bath and a sitting room with double or queen size sofa bed. One suite has a fireplace; the other a woodstove, kitchen and deck.

The farm inn is also one of the few places you can bring your pets. They are not allowed inside but sheltered in a kennel. Equestrians, take heart — horse stabling is also available at the next farm. You are deep in Virginia's piedmont region of horse, cattle and sheep farms. Horseback riding for all ages and degree of proficiency is available. There are fishing and swimming in the spring fed pond and a gazebo for picnics.

Your innkeeper, Beverly Roger Allison, has furnished the delightful abode with antiques and accessories from generations past. She welcomes receptions and private parties. The long, velvet lawn makes for a serene setting for outdoor weddings. Rooms in both the main house and cottage are well-suited for small business meetings.

This good cook will share her recipes. A former missionary, she worked in Central and South America. She currently is associated with the Episcopal Diocese of Honduras, which runs a girls' orphanage in San Padro Sula. Beverly once worked as a news journalist for ABC news in Washington, D.C.

She has now settled in Orange County, created in 1734 and named for William IV of Orange and Anne, Princess Royal of England. Involved in promoting local tourism, Beverly works with local wineries to stage the May Heart of Virginia Wine Festival at Montpelier. Throughout the county are standout historic, cultural and recreational places you may want to visit: Montpelier, home of James and Dolley Madison (only recently opened to the public), Governor Alexander Spotswood's "enchanted castle" (an archeological site), James Madison Museum, Orange County Historical Society Museum, Exchange Hotel (circa 1860), and Chancellorsville, Wilderness and Mine Run battlefields. Charlottesville and its interest-piquing attractions are 25 miles away.

At Wilderness Battlefield is the gravesite of Stonewall Jackson's amputated arm. This is one history lesson your children won't want to miss! The Rapidan River Vineyard is an example of Virginia's newest industry. Barboursville ruins and winery go back to 1814. Four County Players, a local group, performs at the Barboursville Theatre.

You can fish at Lake Orange on Rt.

629. Free Town, near the intersection of Rt. 629 and 669, is the site of an early free black community. Lake Anna, near Rt. 612 and Rt. 522, provides recreational opportunities. A string of old churches makes for a fascinating round; Blue Run Baptist Church dates back to 1769. Along the Rapidan off Rt. 20 lies the Hampstead Archeological District. All told, you can explore 17 historical marker sites or national landmarks. ⌇

*Rt. 3, Box 43*
*Gordonsville, VA 22942*
*703/832-5555*

*90 miles from Washington, D.C.; 67 miles from Richmond. On Rt. 231 between Gordonsville and Somerset. One night's deposit required to reserve rooms. Deposit non-refundable unless cancellation made within 1 week of arrival.*

# BOXWOOD
*Down by the Riverside*

Secluded, quiet, comfortable and somewhat rustic. That's what you will find at Boxwood. Nothing fancy, but a straightforward and warm decor that bids you welcome, as if you were home.

Not only does the hostess live here, but Boxwood is also one of the few B&B's that accommodates young children. Feel free to bring your family. One bedroom has a double bed, crib and single bed with folding sides available.

Built in 1952 as a summer place, the gray river stone and frame home rests on seven acres in a park-like setting surrounded by shrubbery. As you might guess, immense boxwoods on the grounds give the B&B its name. The tranquil atmosphere is enhanced by

neighboring Rawley Springs, where there are paths for lazy strolling or serious hiking.

At Boxwood you can walk out the back door and practically jump into the river. There are honest-to-goodness swimming holes along the river, as well as fine fishing spots.

Boxwood's three terraces, expansive front porch and delightful gazebo provide wonderful sitting areas in the summer. The house and grounds have also become a popular setting for small, less formal weddings and receptions in spring and summer. At the other end of the weather scale, during the winter months you can hibernate inside the high-ceilinged, pine-paneled living room beside the impressive fireplace.

The two-story home is almost lodge-like. Furnishings are comfortable, a la home. Occasional antiques add to the informal spirit.

Bedrooms are spacious. You can opt for a private or shared bath. A sample breakfast might consist of assorted juices, cereals, fresh fruit, English muffins, bagels, apple walnut cake, cream cheese, marmalade, and imported teas or freshly brewed coffee.

Your hostess, Nancy Bondurant Jones, heads the English department at the local high school. She has three biographies to her credit and a fourth book in progress. In her spare moments she collects American art.

Boxwood's shining star is that it's a great place to relax. If you do want to venture off, however, antique shops abound to suit just about any fancy, and country auctions provide regional charm and sometimes even a good bargain! Close by, New Market's Civil War Battlefield Park offers an exceptionally well conceived museum, administered by the Virginia Military Institute. Its extensive grounds and outbuildings provide a good escape for active children.

Also in the vicinity are historic homes and several colleges: James Madison University, Eastern Mennonite College and Bridgewater College. The Skyline Drive crests the mountain range you see in the nearby horizon.

*R.D. 847, Rawley Springs*
*Rt. 1, Box 130*
*Hinton, VA 22831*
*703/867-5772*

*Take U.S. 33 west from I-81 for 13 miles to Rawley Springs. Turn left onto Rt. 847; go 50 yds; Boxwood on right. Reservations by phone only; call after 5 p.m. $10 deposit, no refund.*

# VINE COTTAGE INN
*Comfortable and Cozy*

Your world-traveling innkeepers and resident owners, Wendell and Pat Lucas, know how to make you feel right at home. After living and working abroad, they have chosen to roost next door to the well-known Homestead resort.

They have taken what was more or less a hunting lodge in the Allegheny Mountains and redecorated it in the warm country style of a homey inn. The family-like friendliness of the Lucases complements perfectly the comfortable interiors.

They live at the inn with their two daughters. Uppermost in their minds is allowing their guests to enjoy themselves. They are not fussy or preten-

tious. And they offer you as much personalized attention or privacy as you wish.

The neighboring Homestead is famous for its exquisite dining and world-renowned golf courses. Boutique shops, the spa, skeet field, riding stable, ski slopes, ice-skating rink and trout streams are also alluring.

Many guests of Vine Cottage partake of these activities. Your innkeepers will help you schedule a time on one of the three golf courses or whatever you are interested in.

You can stroll through the little valley village and never have to use your car. There are some nifty eating places, some interesting specialty shops and a

real special outlet, the Bacova Guild Showroom. The factory store features sporting and wildlife gifts made in Bath County and sold throughout the world.

From December through February, Vine Cottage fills its weekends with skiers. The inn offers ski packages, which include two full breakfasts, Friday night welcoming party and Saturday night dinner. The best thing about staying here during a ski outing is returning to a roaring fire in the family room! Groups need to make advanced arrangements with the innkeepers.

Vine Cottage has 13 guest rooms, nine with private baths. You will remember grandma's house with nostalgia when you see the pedestal bath tubs.

The hallway lounges upstairs give you a quiet place to retreat to if your mate sacks out early. In an alcove a chess set is just waiting to be used. Books and magazines are everywhere. You will find a whole wall of good reading downstairs in the family room, where there is also a TV.

The inn serves a complimentary breakfast of cereal, fruit juice, hot breakfast beverages and homemade sticky buns each morning. You will enjoy the informal dining room with its many windows, lovely limestone fireplace and country atmosphere. It's a grand place to meet and socialize with the other guests.

What was once a wrap-around porch is now the dining and family rooms. Another porch has been added and is replete with white wicker rockers to charm every ounce of battle fatigue out of anyone. Typical of the turn-of-the-century architecture, the gabled inn sits in the middle of Virginia's spa region. Ancient thermal springs erupt out of the ground at various sites and since 1750 have provided tourists to this area a gentle form of soothing relaxation.

You are surrounded by the Allegheny mountains, which themselves are a hiker's haven. The colorful foliage makes Bath County exceptionally beautiful in the fall. It is also a hunter's paradise. Eighty-nine percent of the area is forest, with 176,809 acres comprising the George Washington National Forest. The tallest trophy, however, might go to the trout fishing streams — some of America's finest.

Not far away are Gathright Dam and Lake Moomaw, a 12-mile recreational area where you can enjoy boating and swimming. The rivers offer some good canoeing and kayaking. And there is some mighty fine caving in the mountainous terrain.

A newcomer to the area is blossoming into a real treat for music lovers, the Garth Newel Music Concerts. They run every Sunday afternoon from June through August at a rural location halfway between Warm Springs and Hot Springs. The high quality chamber music amid such a bucolic setting may surprise you!

You will have a good time at Vine Cottage. The innkeepers will see to that. ▟

*P.O. Box 918*
*Hot Springs, VA 24445*
*703/839-2422*

*From I-81 at Staunton, take Rt. 254 to Buffalo Gap, Rt. 42 to Goshen, Rt. 39 west to Warm Springs. Rt. 220 south to Hot Springs.*
*Deposit required.*

# NORRIS HOUSE
*A Bit of Virginia's Past*

Two full-time professionals who commute to Washington, D.C., have meticulously restored this 1806 home so that the public could enjoy a taste of Virginia's past. Owners Craig and Amy DeRemer exemplify the gracious hospitality that Virginia is so well-known for. And their personalized touches bring special charm to the stately Norris House Inn, located in the heart of Leesburg's historic district.

The house is named after the Norris family, which had purchased the Federal-style home in 1850 and renovated it in the 1880s. Northern Virginia's foremost architects and builders of the period, the Norris

brothers remodeled the home in the Eastlake style. They added dentil work to the cornice, turned-spindles to the portico and an ornament to the center gable. In the 1820s the house had served as an Episcopal rectory.

Since the DeRemers have owned the home, they have poured hours of research into the color and decorating schemes of their recent remodeling. They tailored Colonial Williamsburg colors to reflect their own tastes. Furnishings are a combination of family pieces, gifts, old furniture from other homes and pieces purchased locally.

The Blue Parlor showcases a china plate on the mantel. It was the Norris's

"Sunday Best." Many remnants of other pieces have been found in the gardens. The Adam's style mantel was carved by the Norris Brothers. A rose-colored clock came from Craig's family; his great-grandmother brought it over from Europe. The 18th century beehive secretary was a gift to Amy from her mother.

The Norris brothers built the wild cherry bookcase in the Music Parlor. Its beautiful patina has been brought out from under layers of paint by the DeRemers' restoration efforts. The Victorian age organ originally came from an Ohio church. You can actually play it if you pull out all the stops to open up the air tubes. The oldest room in the house, the Music Parlor retains the wide pineboard floors of old.

The walnut china hutch and wainscoting embrace the dining room. A mahogany case contains a handwritten letter found during the DeRemers' restoration — it's written by one of the Norris brothers to the other.

A trunk at the end of the bed in the Norris Bedroom is the conversation piece of the inn's largest bedroom. It was the Norris family's traveling trunk; the markings are original.

Named after the first Supreme Court Justice of the United States, the John Jay Bedroom contains an original rope bed that has been converted to accommodate a three-quarters mattress. When the bed was made, the carver had slipped up on a daisy atop the headboard. The mistake lessened the bed's value at that time but today makes it a more valuable antique. Amy's great-grandmother made the yellow quilt from leftover scraps from the dresses of Amy's mother when she was a little girl. Amy named the bedroom after John Jay because she grew up next to his home in Katonah, New York.

The third floor bedrooms had been used by the servants and the Norris children. It was common practice during the Federal period for such rooms to have painted or stenciled floors of lesser pine quality.

Rare mahogany twin beds accent Hannah's Room, named after Hannah Norris and her relative, Hannah Brown Deserda, from across the street. Today, families renting the third floor, use this room for the children.

All of the inn's five guest rooms and two suites are superbly decorated and furnished. Four of the bedrooms contain fireplaces and all are air-conditioned. You have access to the elegant dining room, parlors and sitting rooms. Outside you will enjoy the rambling veranda and well kept garden.

In early evening you are offered complimentary wine, iced tea or cider, when in season. Breakfast includes such treats as fresh melon, lemon muffins, salmon quiche, country ham with raisins and honey, orange juice and a special blend of coffee.

The Norris House Inn is ideal for so many special occasions: holidays, executive retreats, family reunions, weddings or a romantic weekend in Virginia's beautiful hunt country.

The innkeeper can direct you to local "must see's" and recommend the best places to dine. Leesburg is loaded with historic charm. And you are only a stone's throw from the nation's capital.

*108 Loudoun St. SW*
*Leesburg, VA 22075*
*703/777-1806*
*Reservations required, 10a.m.-8p.m.*
*$50 deposit or half the total stay; deposit refunded up to one week prior to coming.*

# FASSIFERN

*Quiet Elegance*

ramed by weeping willows and massive maples, this unusually trimmed home displays such a comfortable setting that you immediately feel right at home. It is two miles from Lexington out in the country on three and a half acres.

Also on the property are a pond and two dependencies, the Ice House and Farm Office. Those buildings, as well as the main house, have been tastefully renovated and furnished with antiques and articles collected by the innkeepers, who traveled around the world during 26 years of military service.

Pat and Jim Tichenor discovered B&B traveling while they were in the

Army. They recently retired and have themselves taken up innkeeping, which they spell with a capital "Ambience."

Their inn, Fassifern, is named after an old Scottish home. Built around 1867, their three-story home features a lovely staircase leading to the second and third floors. An old pump organ nestles beside the fireplace in the living room. Large window space enhances the formal dining room, and each bedroom has its own charm. Inviting areas for lounging and reading are situated throughout the house.

Amenities include bed turn-down with a specially made chocolate left on the pillow, fresh cut flowers in the room

and concierge toiletries. With your room comes an expanded continental breakfast of freshly squeezed juice, fruit in season or fruit compote, homemade breads and muffins, freshly ground coffee, tea, hot chocolate or milk.

Other meals can be gotten in Lexington. Your hosts will serve you refreshments before dinner and help you select a restaurant.

If you are in need of a place to relax, Fassifern will more than meet that need. You can enjoy the serenity of the patio or a quiet walk around the grounds.

Across the street is the Art Farm, where Professor I-Hsiung Ju teaches classes and holds special shows in his gallery. A half mile down the road is the Virginia Horse Center.

Lexington is a veritable treasure of historical sights. Among the most prominent are the Stonewall Jackson House, Robert E. Lee Memorial Chapel and the Marshall Museum at the Virginia Military Institute. One of the oldest colleges in America, Washington and Lee University, is located next to VMI. Other enjoyments in the vicinity include the Blue Ridge Parkway, Natural Bridge and Jefferson National Forest.

*Rt. 5, Box 87*
*Lexington, VA 24450*
*703/463-1013*

*One night deposit required; refundable, less $10, if room re-rented and 10-day notice given. From I-64 Exit 13, take Rt. 39 and go 3/4 mile.*

# HISTORIC COUNTRY INNS

*National Historic Register*

When Susan and Peter Meredith of Norfolk were sending their two sons to Virginia Military Institute (VMI), they had plenty of reasons for trekking to Lexington. They soon realized, however, that Rockbridge County, home of two colleges needed some alternative lodging to the existing motels and hotels.

They embarked on an ambitious project that culminated in the opening first of Alexander-Withrow Inn, then the McCampbell Inn, and most recently, Maple Hall. The owner of Meredith Construction, Peter knew what he was getting into as far as renovation work was concerned. But such sidelines as rounding up cows off Interstate-81 back into Maple Hall's pasture may have been more than he bargained for!

Alexander-Withrow and the Mc-Campbell Inn are on Main Street facing each other, in the heart of Lexington's Historic District. In 1789 William Alexander built a late-Georgian style townhouse, with elegant diapering in the brick work, for his family residence and store. Withrow was the last owner of the home, hence its name. The National Historic Register property saw various periods as a store, a bank and a school. Complete restoration transformed it into a country inn. With chimneys at all four corners, the old building is also a Virginia Historic Landmark.

John McCampbell built his home in 1809. Additions were added around 1816 and 1857. Also on the National Historic Register and a Virginia Historic Landmark, this restored inn formerly housed a jewelry store, doctor's office, the town's telegraph and post office. It once was the Central Hotel, where guests ambled over to a separate building for baths and toilets!

The two in-town inns offer eight suites and 14 rooms, all with individual temperature controls, phone, bath and a refreshment center with refrigerator and hot pot. Wonderful antiques and decorative paintings earmark the decor. Each room has its own look and you can request twin, double or queen beds. For your rocking pleasure there are rocking chairs scattered throughout the verandas.

At McCampbell House guests are served an expanded continental breakfast in the Great Room. During the evening they enjoy a glass of wine. At Alexander-Withrow, local artists and crafts people occupy the groundfloor in a cooperative gallery.

The central office is located in Mc-Campbell. Two rooms may be rented for small gatherings. Don Fredenburg oversees the inns and offers special weekends from time to time, ranging from his Rediscovery Special in January and February for escaping the winter blahs to the Theater Special in summer and Holiday Weekend at Christmas.

Six miles north of Lexington on Route 11, right off I-81, is the Merediths' third property. Encompassed by 56 acres of woods and pasture today, Maple Hall was built around 1850 by John Gibson. The handsome brick home has been charming motorists for years. Surrounded by old boxwoods, the manicured country setting is a very distinguished sight from the highway. Once called Maple Hill Plantation, the Virginia Historic Landmark was bought from Gibson's descendents, restored and made into an inn.

The stately, white-columned home has 12 rooms, 10 with working fireplaces. Each room retains a different character, but they all feature endearing antiques, private bath and separate temperature controls.

Guests can relax on the shaded patio or rock themselves serenely on one of the porches. (Rocking is an old Virginian pastime, if you haven't yet figured out!) A stocked fishing pond and easy walking trails give you a chance to unglue the kinks out of "travel-legs." Maple Hall has a tennis court and swimming pool for guests.

A most inviting area is the enclosed Garden Room, one of the dining rooms that serves a la carte dinner Wednesday through Saturday evenings. The inn features a gourmet brunch on Sundays, April through October.

The restored Guest House, across the patio, gives you a place to reserve your own cozy quarters. A non-smoking area, it includes a living room, kitchen and three bedrooms with baths. It is suitable for a single guest, a family or as a mini-conference center. Maple Hall itself is a good place for small business and social functions. The inn can accommodate seminars, luncheons and gala lawn receptions.

All three inns are a poignant indicator that you are in the thick of history. Eastern Virginia has its Williamsburg, Central Virginia its Fredericksburg and the Shenandoah Valley its Lexington. There is so much history oozing out of this unique town, history buffs will salivate.

*Continued next page*

## Historic Country Inns, Continued

The illustrious Stonewall Jackson had a home here. VMI (another National Historic Landmark) operates one of the best museums you will ever find. It honors George C. Marshall, World War II Army Chief of Staff and author of the Marshall Plan. Robert E. Lee, one of the few leaders America ever had that historians have yet to dig up any dirt on, spent his last years here presiding over Washington and Lee University. Next door to VMI, W&L is the nation's sixth oldest college. Lee Chapel and Museum is a National Historic Landmark on the campus. Sam Houston, later of Tennessee and Texas fame, was born nearby in Lexington.

You can walk the streets of Lexington and easily think you've happened upon a 19th century village. Two summer theaters of increasing renown, the Lime Kiln Arts (outdoor) and Henry Street Playhouse, provide some great entertainment. There are some interesting little shops and Lexington is now host to the Virginia Horse Center.

Not far away is Wades Mill, a 19th century flour mill, the farm and home site of Cyrus McCormick, who invented the reaper. Natural Bridge lies in the opposite direction and the Blue Ridge Parkway runs parallel to I-81. What the Chessie trail is to hikers, the Maury River is to canoers. And perhaps one of the grandest spots of all is Goshen Pass, revered by natives and students alike. Tubing and fishing are regular occurrences there, but many folks go simply for the beauty of the mountain laurel and rhododendron.

*11 North Main St.*
*Lexington, VA 24450*
*703/463-2044*

*Either exit off I-81 into Lexington.*
*Maple Hall is off Exit 53 at Rt. 11 north.*
*Deposit required, refundable*
*10 days before arrival date.*
*Corporate rate available.*

*Along the Blue Ridge Parkway, voted by travel writers as the nation's most popular scenic roadway.*

# FORT LEWIS LODGE

*In the Wilds*

eep within Virginia's Allegheny Mountains, Fort Lewis Lodge preserves 3200 private acres of spectacular scenery, rushing mountain streams, graceful whitetail deer, great home cooking and real mountain leisure. The lodge sits at the heart of a working grain and cattle farm that was originally carved from the wilderness in 1755 as a frontier outpost and has remained virtually unaltered for over 200 years.

Ten years ago John and Caryl Cowden moved from Dayton, Ohio, to manage the farm that has been in John's family since the 1950s. John brought with him a degree in agronomy and interests in construction, woodworking,

mountain biking, fishing, hunting and gardening. Caryl came with a background in childhood education and interests in cooking, perennial flower gardening, hiking and other sports.

Along with operating the farm, restoring the old red-brick manor house as their home, and raising three children in the process, John and Caryl have spent a great deal of time restoring the Lewis gristmill dating back to 1850 and building the new guest lodge.

Over two miles of the winding Cowpasture River, which once powered the gristmill, divide this fertile valley of cultivated fields, meadows and big hardwood forests. Close to the lodge is a swimming hole (complete with skip-

ping stones) for guests to enjoy throughout the summer months. Guests can also sport fish (catch and release) along the Cowpasture River for small mouth bass and trout. Keepers are limited to trophy class fish. Rock bass are common and a lot of fun for children. Several state-stocked trout streams are nearby. Miles of well marked trails and old abandoned logging roads are also yours to explore on the property.

The spacious two-story lodge features a large "gathering room" framed with massive beams of oak and walnut. An enclosed stairway leading to the top of an adjoining silo serves as an observation tower for a spectacular view "in the round" of the grounds below. The lodge has 12 bedrooms with private or semi-private baths. Much of the furniture is handmade by local craftsmen from wood cut on the property — walnut, cherry, red oak and butternut.

The Lewis Mill "Country Kitchen" serves all three meals and is housed in the four-story gristmill. The hand-hewn post and beam framing with exposed interior clapboard on a thick stone foundation all add to the warm and rustic atmosphere of the dining room.

Meals, all three of which are included in the room rate, are a parade of dishes too good to resist with "homemade everything." A full country breakfast includes freshly baked breads, eggs, sausage, bacon and seasonal fruits, or may include French toast drenched with locally-made maple syrup. You can lunch in the lodge or take out a box lunch. Buffet dinners, best described as "country with a flair," offer fresh vegetables from the garden.

The summer guest season runs from May 15 through mid-October. The hunting season at Fort Lewis for deer and turkey then follows and runs through December. Spring gobbler season resumes in the spring, from April to mid-May.

Camping is another added attraction at Fort Lewis. With advance booking the lodge will outfit overnight campouts high up on the mountain or along the river. Other activities are river tubing, spelunking, observing and photographing wildlife. Children will enjoy a trip to the barnyard to collect eggs or to try their hand at milking a cow.

*Millboro, VA 24460*
*703/925-2314*

*From I-81 (Staunton): 254 west, go straight onto 42 west at Buffalo Gap, go straight onto 39 west at Millboro Springs, right Rt. 678, left 625.*
*Deposit of one night's stay required, refundable for cancellations received 14 days prior to coming; otherwise, $10 service fee retained if room re-rented. Please note: unlike other inns, three meals are included in the room-rate (American Plan).*

# INN AT MONTROSS
*Serving Travelers Since 1683*

History is for real here. In fact, a copy of the original handwritten grant for an "ordinary" hangs on display at the inn. In 1683 the justices of Westmoreland County in the Northern Neck granted John Minor permission to have a tavern on the site, as long as he served no spirits while the court was in session!

The building was actually built prior to 1683. Thomas Lee of Stratford Hall, an uncle of Robert E. Lee, frequently visited the inn during his tenure as a Burgess. The Spence family took over the tavern in 1730. Down through the ages the building has seen service as a hotel, home for the elderly and an inn.

Around 1790 the building was destroyed and then rebuilt. Remnants of

the original foundation are visible today from the wine cellar, once again serving as "John Minor's Ordinary."

England has always had a love affair with its inns, and that is where many American innkeepers picked up the idea. So leave it to an Englishman, with an inbred appreciation of innkeeping, to buy the Inn at Montross. Michael Longman, the English transplant, has been an avid inn-goer with his wife Eileen. They are both travelers at heart and have put to use the best of what they've encountered over the years. He is a former banker and she a nursing consultant to the state of Maryland.

The inn is about the only establishment in town. Montross is rather remote, but the dining experience draws

a steady flow of customers. Two attractive dining rooms serve a fantastic menu at surprisingly reasonable prices. For starters you may select oysters on the half-shell, smoked salmon, mushroom caps, escargot chef Michael and other festive appetizers. You have the option of a soup course.

Entrees are cooked to order. Dishes include roast prime rib of beef, a filet specialty, London broil, surf and turf, lobster tails (which come with 10 1/2 easy lessons for how to eat the crustacean that has made Montross's reputation), crab cakes in the Maryland style, crab imperial, shrimp and crab Newburg, catch of the day, roast duck, boneless breast of chicken, choice veal and fettucini Alfredo. For dessert you get to choose from a pastry cart or ice cream with your favorite liqueur.

You are between the Potomac and Tappahannock rivers, which feed out into the Chesapeake Bay not far away. You have to know that the seafood is not simply good here. It's great! Don't miss out.

Lodgers receive their continental-plus breakfast free of charge. The breakfast takes in fresh fruit and southern specialties and is served to guests on the cheerful dining room porch. Guests may order a full breakfast if they wish.

The restaurant serves the public for lunch and dinner. Recently opened, the Colonial Pub on the lower level and the Pub Room serve pre- and post-dinner drinks.

Overnighters will enjoy the guest rooms. All six have a private bath, fragrant toiletries, and individual climate control for your personal comfort. Four-poster beds highlight each room — some are antiques, some are reproductions.

The overall decor reflects a combination of tastes of the owners. Some of the furniture is from their personal collection, and accessories include a mixture of primitive and modern art, porcelains and other accents.

Common areas are a television lounge and living room on the main floor. A magnificent grand piano dominates the main floor and guests are free to tickle the ivories. Occasionally a guest artist will be on hand to set the mood.

Some of the things you will remember about your experience here: hot coffee or tea served in a clear glass like an Irish coffee mug; in the spring, fresh asparagus picked from the local garden; extra pillows in your rooms; colored sheets to match the decorating scheme; friendly innkeepers; brandy snifters and chocolate mint cookies for a nightcap in your room.

Area attractions include the birthplace of one of Virginia's finest statesmen of all times, Robert E. Lee. His uncle, who often stopped by Montross in the early days, built Stratford Hall in the 1720s for his father Richard Henry Lee, known to his colleagues as "Light Horse" Harry Lee.

George Washington's birthplace is

also nearby. The National Monument gives you detailed insight to America's early history. Ingleside Winery welcomes touring visitors and will give you a taste or two! Westmoreland State Park and Westmoreland Berry Farm are in the area. An unforgettable excursion is a day trip by ferry to Smith or Tangier Islands, where Elizabethan English is still spoken.

*Courthouse Square*
*Montross, VA 22520*
*804/493-9097*

*115 miles from Baltimore; 60 miles from Richmond. Take Rt. 360 through Tappahannock to Warsaw, then Rt. 3 west, if you come from the south. From the north, take I-95 or Rt. 301 to Rt. 3. Night's deposit required; refunded less $10 service charge if cancellation 3 days before arrival.*

# PUMPKIN HOUSE INN

*Family Home Place*

Yrou know you've arrived when you see the pumpkins painted on the corn crib across the road from the inn. The B & B's handsome portico and stately, squarish facade tempt you to think you'll be staying in a Greek Revival farmhouse. You may decide you've wandered into the Victorian age once you glimpse the inside. The Pumpkin House Inn was built in 1847 and resembles other area homes. Whatever the inn's style, one thing for sure: host Tom Kidd and Liz Umstott make you feel right at home.

Family heirlooms, antique furniture on consignment, stenciling around the ceilings, attention to decorative details, oriental and braided rugs, and lush wines, teals, greens and golds accentuate the interiors. Tom and Liz have done a class act in preserving their homeplace, which their father had bought in 1947.

The Gold Room, a first floor guest room, has a fireplace, an armoire, an antique bed and a chandelier. The table was made by their grandfather. Victorian furnishings fill the sitting area at the end of the foyer. An exquisite marble-top sideboard sits in the front of the foyer. Overhead hangs a large, original kerosene lamp and an original spandrel, embellished by recently-added Victorian stenciling.

One level down is the Country Guest Room, walled with cozy brick on one side and situated next to a lounge equipped with TV, library, information center and fireplace.

On the second floor the Cat Room, the most popular bedroom in the house, features a high-arched, canopy bed with a white, hand-tied top. Stenciled, foot-high, black cats with white faces peer down from their ceiling perch. Behind the door sits a cat with a mouse in its mouth!

Three bedrooms have private baths with showers. Four rooms share two baths. A black notebook in each room lists the furnishings that are for sale.

Breakfasts are a treat. Features are pumpkin muffins, of course, pastries, fruit compote and cereals. You'll love the coffee, spiced with cinnamon.

During the warm months, you'll find quiet delight in sitting outside in the side yard under the big trees and surveying the farm. North River (good fishing under the bridge) and Cook's Creek frame the farm's borders. You can view Massanutten Peak, where you'll find skiing in the winter months. Horseback riding is nearby and canoeing 45 minutes away on the Shenandoah River. You can traipse around the inn's 43 acres or hike the many trails in the George Washington National Forest and along the Skyline Drive. Some of the best antiquing anywhere is along Route 11.

If you are a Civil War buff, you'll be enthralled. Union General Sheridan stayed here when his troops holed up in the barn during their raids in the Shenandoah Valley. The inn displays one of its finds: brass crossed cannons, Union artillery insignia for the cap. Pumpkin House is smack in the middle of Civil War action and not far from the Civil War Battlefield in New Market.

Situated between Harrisonburg and Staunton, the inn is surrounded by colleges: Bridgewater, Eastern Mennonite, James Madison University, Blue Ridge Community College and Mary Baldwin.

*Rt. 2, Box 155*
*Mount Crawford, VA 22841*
*703/434-6963*

*One night's deposit required; cancellation within 48 hrs. Check-in 4 p.m.; check-out 11 a.m.*

# WIDOW KIP'S COUNTRY INN

*Glow of Bedroom Fireplaces*

You guessed it! A widow named Rosemary Kip owns this Mt. Jackson vestige of the past. In the fall, you're liable to arrive and find your host cooking apple butter in the kitchen. The spiced fragrance permeates the two-story, gray-framed and maroon-shuttered Victorian home situated near Mill Creek, a fork of the Shenandoah River.

This 1830 homestead rests on seven rural acres, where you view the Shenandoah Valley, George Washington National Forest and cows grazing 10 feet from the swimming pool.

The inn extends its offerings beyond the main home to two cottages. One, which was originally the chicken coop, has two bedrooms, a kitchen and bath; the other — a former wash house — has a cozy bedroom and bath. Bikes are provided for a carefree ride through the apple orchard country to the Shenandoah Caverns nearby.

Everything inside the lace-curtained home is for sale, even the canopy bed you sleep in. You'll discover top-notch antiques, such as the sleigh bed, 8-foot Lincoln beds, ornate Partner's desk and intricate armoires. Locally handcrafted, multicolor quilts are for purchase, as well as the multitude of other crafts and collectibles found in the Courtyard Gift Shop. The appealing interiors sport a colonial look with Victorian overtones.

The main house has a first-floor bedroom, a fireplaced common room where guests can play backgammon or checkers, and four guest rooms upstairs. All six bedrooms have woodburning fireplaces, and five rooms come with private baths. Two staff members assist the owner, who managed New York City and Washington, D.C., clubs for 25 years until her recent migration to the Shenandoah Valley.

An excellent cook, Rosemary will start your day with a full country breakfast of apple juice (the Shenandoah Valley is famed for its apples), eggs, homemade sausage, biscuits, nut muffins, apple butter and coffee. If you prefer to eat lunch or dinner at Widow Kip's, the inn sells a split chicken or steak with barbeque sauce, coleslaw and biscuits. You are welcome to use the gas grill in the courtyard and dine on the side porch. Also available, for a modest charge, is a lighter menu of sandwiches, fruits, ice cream and beverages. You may want to pack a picnic!

You can slow down to a snail's pace here. Stacks of books fill the living room and bedrooms. Rockers await you on the side porch. A 32-foot swimming pool is out back. Weekend auctions, hikes, canoeing, skiing, craft fairs, golf, caverns, vineyards, bikes and picnics will vie for your time. The Shenandoah River snakes through the vicinity and is a source of outdoor pleasure.

*Rt. 1, Box 117*
*Mt. Jackson, VA 22842*
*703/477-2400*

*I-81, Exit 69 to Rt. 11 south. Go 1.3 miles; right onto Rt. 263, left on 698. Pay upon arrival. Check-in 2 p.m.; check-out, 12 noon.*

# MAYHURST INN
*Captivating Architecture*

hat a gem — this Italiante Victorian mansion has no equal. It's movie-set perfect and has most deservedly been placed on the National Register of Historic Places, as well as earned respect as a Virginia Historic Landmark.

Simply put, Mayhurst is a work of art. The vivid gingerbread shines with luster, as the owners Stephen and Shirley Ramsey slowly piece it together to recapture the past prize.

Col. John Willis, great-nephew of President James Madison, built this one-of-a-kind home in 1859-60. Uncle James, by the way, lived in a home,

Montpelier, further out in the country. His home eventually found its way into the Dupont estate and has long been the site of annual steeplechases. The Madison home has now been transferred to the Historic Trust and for the first time opened its doors to the public. When you are visiting Mayhurst, put Montpelier at the top of your "to see" list.

Mayhurst will lodge you in one of its six guest rooms, each with a private bath and many harboring fireplaces. Double arched windows lend an aristocratic aura to your quarters.

The focal point of all this fanciful ar-

chitecture is the oval-spiral staircase soaring up four floors to a rooftop gazebo. And what has more charm than a gazebo! Antiques vie for the glory of the rooms. At Mayhurst they are exceptional in quality. You will want to rummage through the antique barn out back, where you can purchase your find of the century.

During the Civil War, Gen. A.P. Hill commanded his Northern Virginia army from this post. He hosted Gen. Stonewall Jackson here. Today the estate comprises 36 acres of aged oaks, cedars (you'll always find these aromatic evergreens at Virginia's old homesteads) and magnolias. You can fish in the pond, explore the fields, linger along some trails or picnic in solitude.

Orange County is also the site of President Zachary Taylor's home, Montebello. You are a half-hour from the home of another Virginian president, Thomas Jefferson's Monticello. Charlottesville, of course, is also home of the University of Virginia. Surprisingly enough, you're only thirty minutes from another center of history, Fredericksburg. Richmond is one hour away and Washington, D.C., two hours.

You are served a southern country breakfast each morning, and afternoon tea on the weekends. On Saturdays you can order dinner for $15. Midweek business travelers are offered discounted rates.

*P.O. Box 707*
*Orange, VA 22960*
*703/672-5597*

*On Rt. 15, 1/4 mile south of Orange.*

# HIGH STREET INN
*Victorian in Old Towne*

There are more reasons than you might realize to come to this old Virginia city and stay in this Queen Anne mansion in the oldest part of town. The settlement that became Petersburg was founded in 1645 as a frontier fort and trading post, so you really are in some old territory with a real past.

The inn is located in the Old Towne District, which is on the National Historic Register. John A. Gill, a prosperous wholesale grocer who had nine children, built the home in 1895. The family lived there for about 30 years, and then the building was used commercially until 1985.

Bruce and Candace Noe purchased the home with an intent to restore the yellow-brick, Victorian period home and use it as a bed and breakfast inn. The exterior is set off by a turret in the front and balanced in the back with a round, two-story porch.

The Noes worked through all phases of the restoration, from stripping old wallpaper and paint to hanging new wall coverings in each of the 17 rooms. They carefully selected every antique, oriental rug, painting and accessory with the pleasure of their future guests in mind. As a result, the beds are some of the most exquisite you will find anywhere!

The innkeepers followed an eclectic design scheme in decorating the five guest rooms: each represents a different period, from Federal to Eastlake. The windows are treated with lace curtains, oriental rugs carpet the original wood floors and old, claw-foot tubs were put in all of the bathrooms.

The Eastlake Room features a turret alcove with table and chairs and a matching set of marble-topped Eastlake furniture from Philadelphia.

In the Rococo Room you will find one of the prize beds, hand carved in walnut, and an unusual table with inlaid mother-of-pearl. A sleigh bed dominates the Empire Room, warmed by a corner fireplace. Hand-carved, twin pineapple beds fill the Federal Room. You are treated to a queen-size, hand-carved walnut bed with an eight-foot headboard in the Renaissance Room. A sitting room furnished in wicker forms a suite with this bedroom.

Guests have free reign of the parlor, sunroom and dining room downstairs. There are more antiques amid the 19th century look. Twin Rococo Revival settees, a rosewood melodian and a very unusual gas-burning fireplace highlight the parlor. The sunroom extends below the pillared balcony, which can be noticed on the side of the house. There are 216 panes in the sunroom window! And the dining room is no less a work of art. It is furnished with a Jacobean Revival banquet table, Sheraton banquet table and a matching set of eight Sheraton chairs with their original needlepoint seats.

You are served complimentary afternoon tea or sherry. The parlor and sunroom offer TV, stereo, books and games. Classic and foreign language films are available for viewing. In the morning your host serves freshly brewed coffee, home-baked muffins, croissants and Smithfield ham biscuits, which you may enjoy in your room or in the dining room.

Old Towne is a good example of the city's renewed spirit and will to survive. Once the heart of 19th century industry along the banks of the Appomattox River, Old Towne now houses antique shops, craft boutiques and restaurants. An open air Farmers Market cloisters around an historic, hexagonal structure.

Nearby is Gen. Robert E. Lee's headquarters, which he used while he was making his last stand before his retreat to Appomattox. During the Civil War, which Virginians call "The War Between the States," Petersburg's rivers and railways served as the military and economic lifeline of the Confederacy. They also made the city a strategic target for the Union forces. The 10-month siege of Petersburg was the longest and deadliest battle ever fought on American soil. The city lost much of its glory. Today the Siege Museum recaptures the heritage that once belonged to the proud city.

Centre Hill Mansion portrays the architectural evolution from 1823 through 1901 and serves as headquarters for the Virginia chapter of the Victorian Society.

Blandford Church is in a category all by itself. It has 15 stained-glass windows personally designed by Louis Comfort Tiffany and is one of only five buildings anywhere in which every window is an original Tiffany creation. Built in 1735, the church adjoins a graveyard where the oldest headstone dates back to 1702. It is here that Memorial Day was first started.

The U.S. Army Quartermaster Museum is also located in Petersburg, inside Fort Lee. Artifacts date back to Revolutionary War when Petersburg enjoyed a thriving tobacco trade. The Petersburg National Battlefield Park is the actual site of Lee's last stand before Appomattox.

High Street Inn is within 30 minutes of downtown Richmond or the James River plantations. It is within 45

minutes of Kings Dominion, and within an hour of Colonial Williamsburg and Busch Gardens.  ⁌

*405 High St.*
*Petersburg, VA 23803*
*804/733-0505*

*From I-85 or I-95, take Exit 3,*

*Washington St. Go to fifth light; turn right onto Market St. Go to second light, turn left onto High Street. Inn is a block and a half on right. Offstreet parking available to inn's left.*

# BENSONHOUSE OF RICHMOND

*In The Fan*

The historic district that is perhaps most well-known in Richmond for its restorations is the area called The Fan. Not far from downtown, this neighborhood community is flourishing, with a population blend of the older and the younger generation. You will delight in walking the streets and eyeing the unique homes with the tiny, well-cared-for gardens.

Nostalgia punctuated with a good face lift.

Central to the city of Richmond, The Fan is a super place for an overnight bed and breakfast guest: Summerhouse is well-positioned and will please your every fanciful whim. Large and gracious, the 1908 house sparkles with revived life given it recently by its new owners, a highly creative couple.

Located on Richmond's famed Monument Avenue, the house suffered heavy damage years ago. The owners, both working professionals, have had the millwork faithfully reproduced. It shows up magnificently around the brightly colored walls, fireplaces and windows. The detailed highlights smartly set off the home. In 1986 Summerhouse was featured on The Fan Christmas Tour.

You make reservations at this B&B through the Bensonhouse of Richmond reservation service. There are several offerings. Twin and queen-bedded guest rooms adjoin one another on the third floor. A bath and wet bar come with the accommodations. You can look out over the city for some eye-catching views.

The second floor offers a queen-bedded room and private bath. An optional suite with fireplace connects the room.

Summerhouse makes available a special package for anniversary celebrations or honeymoons. Wine, champagne, fresh flowers and breakfast brought to the room on silver service add to your memories.

The owners have renovated five Richmond homes and love collecting art, antiques and new friends. Refurbished from top to bottom, the Richmond bed and breakfast house will serve you comfortably.

You are within walking distance of the Virginia Museum of Fine Arts and numerous restaurants. As you poke along Monument Avenue, you will notice all the statues. It is one of the few historic avenues in the country. To keep the district intact, an architectural review commission controls all renovation efforts.

Other points of interest include the State Capitol, which contains some lovely, historic pieces of art; the Edgar Allan Poe Museum; various walking tours; and Civil War Battlefields.

Richmond is one and a half hour's drive from Charlottesville, two and a half hour's drive from Washington, D.C., and an hour from Williamsburg. Bensonhouse runs one of the most efficent reservation services for bed and breakfast establishments, and has other listings within a two-hour radius of Richmond. A leader in the field, Lyn Benson is highly selective in the properties she handles and regularly inspects them. She has also had firsthand experience in renovating a B&B, as she has taken her own home down to the bare bones before restoring it to a high quality establishment.

*2036 Monument Ave.*
*Richmond, VA 23220*
*804/648-7560*

*10-day cancellation deposit return, less $20 service charge.*

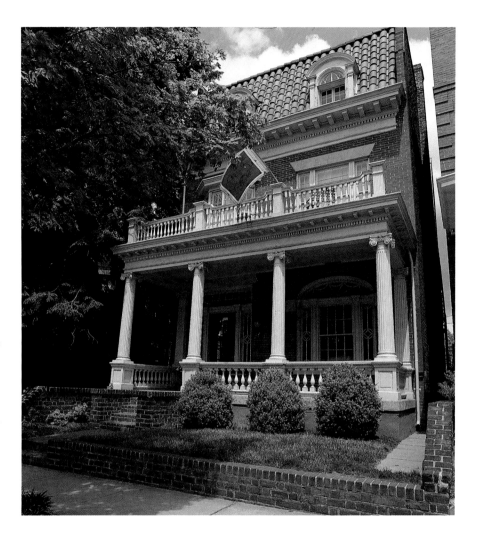

What a wonderful alternative to big-city hotel lodging if you're coming to Richmond! What a great excuse for even coming to Virginia's capital city. You are minutes away, if you're on business, from the downtown district. If you're on a sightseeing excursion, you are in the heart of a real neighborhood with special historic charm.

St. John's Church, where Patrick Henry uttered his famous "Give me liberty, or give me death" speech, is right across the street. There are battlefield parks and James River plantations along nearby Route 5. The Edgar Allan Poe Museum, Virginia State Capitol Museum, John Marshall House, the White House of the Confederacy and Shockoe Slip with its bevy of popular restaurants, shops and boutiques are all cause for staying at nearby Catlin-Abbott House.

The well-appointed home was built in 1845 for William Catlin by his slave William Mitchell, one of the finest brick masons in Richmond then. Mitchell was also the father of Maggie Walker,

America's first woman bank president. In 1850 when Catlin built another home on East Broad Street for his third wife, he rented out the first home. A six-room addition was built in 1870 to accommodate boarders.

Your innkeepers are the owners, Dr. and Mrs. James L. Abbott, who live in the addition. Antiques, family heirlooms, fresh flowers and working fireplaces welcome you. The bedrooms are filled with period furniture, canopied four-poster beds, large armoires and oriental rugs. You may find the comforts exceed those in your own home — triple sheeting, goose down pillows, sherry and mints, nightly turn-down service.

You are served coffee or tea in the mornings at your room. You come downstairs to a full breakfast in the fashionably 19th century designed dining room: juice or fresh fruit in season, sausage and tea. Breakfast is brought to your room, if you so desire.

Especially delightful is the second-story veranda off from the rooms and the lovely courtyard-type backyard.

Colorful impatiens lining the walk make a stunning sight.

Richmond makes an ideal springboard from which to take day excursions to Virginia's most popular tourist attractions. When you exhaust the sites and doings of the capital city, you can head east to Colonial Williamsburg, an hour away, or west to Thomas Jefferson's grand old home near Charlottesville. Monticello is about an hour's drive.

*2304 East Broad St.*
*Richmond, VA 23223*
*804/780-3746*

*From I-95, southbound: take Exit 11, 3rd St. ramp, to 5th traffic light (Broad St.), turn left and proceed east, inn on left. From I-64, westbound, take 5th St. Exit, downtown, to Broad St., turn left. Deposit on first night required, non-refundable.*
*Check-in 3 p.m.; check-out 12 noon.*

*Charlottesville's Monticello, one of the nation's most superbly designed homes.*

# MARY BLADON HOUSE
*Victorian and Sociable*

nnkeeper Sally Pfister has painstakingly refurbished a late 1880s home in Old Southwest, Roanoke's historic neighborhood. She is a delightful hostess and greets her guests with warm enthusiasm. You will feel as though you've known her for years.

Her corner Victorian home is 20 minutes from the airport and within a brisk walk of downtown, so it's ideal for traveling business people. Roanoke boasts one of the oldest outdoor markets in the nation. Center in the Square is located on the market. That

unique building houses the museums of art, history and science. Within its walls also are a modern planetarium, playhouse and Visitor's Center. The house is a convenient springboard to the Blue Ridge Parkway, which goes through Roanoke five minutes away and connects near the Mill Mountain Zoo.

The home is named after the wife and daughter of the second owner. As early as 1892, "Mother Bladon" took in boarders. Her husband, like most men in Roanoke during that era, worked for Norfolk and Western Railroad. The

Transportation Museum 10 blocks away preserves that past. Seven owners later, the Elizabethan Victorian house retains many quality construction appointments of its time: high ceilings, ornate fireplaces, brass light fixtures, crown and bullseye moldings, and spacious porches.

The works of several Virginia artists hang proudly on the walls and are for sale. Furnishings are period antiques and local craft pieces.

Sally lives on the premises with her well-behaved cats and dogs, who are discouraged from straying from her quarters unless a guest requests otherwise.

Your innkeeper writes poetry and designs floral arrangements, when she's not flea-market shopping for the perfect accent piece. Her main interest, however, is people, which accounts for her royal guest treatment. A good cook, she may try out a new recipe on you and ask for your frank opinion — add it or not to the extensive breakfast menu? Parlor tea is included in your rate.

You are invited to enjoy a glass of sherry on the porch or take it to your room with a good book. The Mary Bladon House is central to a number of fine restaurants. Maps and menus are kept at the house to help your decision-making. You are a pleasant day's drive from any of the state's historical sites.

You may want to walk through the neighborhood and observe how other period homes are being restored. Highland Park, two blocks away, is home for the Alexander-Gish House, possibly the oldest surviving structure in Roanoke.

With advance notice Sally will host bridal teas and showers. Sensitive to the needs of parents without partners and senior citizens, she offers a 10 percent discount to these groups.

*381 Washington Ave. SW*
*Roanoke, VA 24016*
*703/344-5361*

*I-581 to Elm Ave. Exit, westbound. Left at Franklin Rd., right onto Washington. $45 deposit required; refunds less $5 for 2-day cancellation notice.*

# MANOR AT TAYLOR'S STORE

*Best  of  Both  Worlds*

This historic, 100-acre estate lies in the picturesque foothills of the Blue Ridge Mountains, between Roanoke and Smith Mountain Lake.

Taylor's Store dates to 1799, when Skelton Taylor, a First Lieutenant in Virginia's Bedford Militia, established his trading post at this site. The general store and ordinary (a term used in the olden days for "inn") served the local community and early settlers traveling west on the Old Warwick Road. In 1818 it became a U.S. Post Office. Taylor's Store, a prominent landmark on early maps of the region, no longer stands today. The original manor house, built in the early 1800s on a prosperous

tobacco plantation, remains as a nicely restored blend of old and new.

The Manor, replete with period antiques, has four guest rooms, each with a private bath. Whether you select a room with fireplace, garden porch, or balcony, each is a romantic interlude from another era. All guests may enjoy the formal Victorian parlor with grand piano, the rustic slate-floored "great room," the billiard room, the fully equipped guest kitchen, the exercise room, and the hot tub. A sunroom with lots of windows has views of the lovely countryside. The entire mansion is centrally air-conditioned. This is truly the best of both worlds!

A cozy cottage on the estate features

three bedrooms, two baths, a fully equipped kitchen, stone fireplace, and a huge deck with fabulous views of the five ponds. This offers families or groups traveling together a comfortable, casual atmosphere and a private outside paradise to enjoy.

Meals at the inn are a very special treat. In addition to gourmet quality cuisine, all meals are "heart healthy" and follow the American Heart Association guidelines. Lavish breakfast selections include whole grain pancakes and waffles, quiches, crepes, and souffles, served with fresh fruit. An "innkeeper's dinner" is also available with advance reservations. This is a full five-course meal with the entree varying nightly, crowned by a house specialty dessert, such as "crepes au chocolat with raspberry Cointreau sauce."

Your hosts, Lee and Mary Lynn Tucker, pursue careers as a pathologist and nurse; on the side they enjoy music, art, hiking, skiing, fishing, raising their Newfoundland dogs, and of course, renovation, antiques and cooking. Their easy-going hospitality creates an atmosphere of "being at home" for guests.

The Taylor's Store estate offers an endless array of things to see and do. You can canoe or fish the ponds, hike most anywhere, and picnic as you wish. A swimming area is under construction. You may also play billiards, darts, croquet, volleyball, and, when it snows, cross-country ski. A five-minute drive takes you to Virginia's premier lake, Smith Mountain Lake, which offers infinite recreational resources: boating of all kinds, fishing, golf, swimming, tennis and fine dining. Roanoke, a 20-minute drive, showcases the Mill Mountain Zoo, Farmer's Market and Center-in-the -Square with its host of cultural activities. The Blue Ridge Parkway is also a 20-minute drive away and provides access to panoramic views, Peaks of Otter and Mabry Mill.

*Route 1, Box 533*
*Wirtz, VA 24184*
*703/721-3951*

*Located on Rt. 122, 1.6 miles north of Burnt Chimney (intersection 116 and 122) and 3.8 miles south of Booker T. Washington National Monument. Look for brick columns at driveway stating "Taylor's Store, circa 1799."*
*One night's deposit to confirm reservations; fully refundable up until 10 days prior to arrival date. Refunds after that dependent upon re-occupation of accommodation.*
*Check-in 4 - 10 p.m. ; check-out by 11 a.m., unless special arrangements are made.*

# ISLE AT WIGHT
*With a Personal Touch*

Three ardent innkeepers blend their flair for life with a most winsome B&B, anchored near the shores of the James River in Smithfield, where homes date back to the 1750s. In concert with the inn is an antique shop that specializes in fine period furniture, glassware, 18th and 19th century clocks, and accessories.

Sam Earl, retired NASA engineer who worked with America's space program for 35 years, is a master clock maker and expert in antiques. He owns one of the best antique clock collections in the Commonwealth. He lives near the inn with his wife, a librarian, in the King-Atkinson house built in 1790 and furnished with antiques of the period. They have made numerous trips to England to buy antiques for the business.

Marcella Hoffman manages the inn after leaving a career in retailing. She makes guests feel at home with her friendly personality and talent for good cooking. Her husband often lends a helping hand at the inn.

Bob Hart, world traveler, photographer and advertising professional, brings more than business management to the inn and antique shop. His infectious good humor reinforces the friendly, relaxed atmosphere at Isle of Wight, so it's no wonder why the inn is a popular place for tourists and business people. In the 15 years he worked for the Baptist Foreign Mission Board, the man who likes to tell stories and make people laugh traveled to more than 50 countries. He has photographed Presidents Gerald Ford, Jimmy Carter and Lyndon Johnson. The Caroline County native fell in love with the old seaport town nine years ago while passing through and now serves on the town council. He and his wife, who keeps the books for the inn, live in a nearby, restored, 17-room Colonial Revival mansion built around the turn of the century and overlooking the Pagan River.

Surrounded by more than 60 old Colonial and Victorian homes, the Isle of Wight is a perfect springboard from which to take a walking tour of the area. St. Luke's Church, erected in 1632 and the oldest English speaking church in America, is a National Shrine open daily to the public. The inn is just seven miles from the south end of the James River Bridge on Route 10 west, so you are in good position to sightsee the famous James River plantations. Williamsburg, Jamestown, Yorktown, Virginia Beach, Norfolk, Hampton and Fort Monroe are a 20-30 minute drive away. You can take a ferry across the James to the Historic Triangle. Ten minutes from the inn are Chippokes Plantation, a Surry farm that has been in continuous operation since 1619, and Bacon's Castle.

The Isle of Wight was completely renovated into a luxurious inn with all the modern amenities in 1984. All 10 rooms offer air conditioning, private bath, cable TV with HBO, and telephone. Rates include a continental breakfast of coffee, juice, ham biscuits and Danish.

Rooms are individually decorated, with accents of chair railing, wallpaper and queen-sized, four-poster beds made of mahogany. There are several large suites with fireplaces; the honeymoon suite also features a jacuzzi. For the physical fitness hound, the grounds contain a walking and jogging trail.

*1607 South Church St.*
*Smithfield, VA 23430*
*804/357-3176*

*One mile east of downtown*
*Smithfield on Rt. 10, near*
*south end of James River Bridge.*

# THE CONYERS HOUSE

*Hunt Set Favorite*

**Sperryville**

hether you ride or not, you will find the weekend or Wednesday foxhunt a colorful spectacle. Dressed in reds and blacks, 30 some riders and 50 some hounds from the Rappahannock Hunt Club canter off through the field from October to March. Larry LeHew, Master of Fox Hounds (the left rider pictured in the foreground), leads the way. He has held that elected position for 10 years. The gent pictured to the right of him is Col. John Lyle, another Rappahannock Hunt faithful.

"We begin cubbing after Labor Day," equestrienne - innkeeper Sandra Cartwright-Brown explains. "That is, we start a month of informal hunting prac-

tice, where the experienced hounds can teach the younger ones."

The formal hunting then commences, with the Opening Meet and the Blessing of the Hounds on the last Saturday in October.

With all the pageantry and flair, The Conyers House serves as an ideal backdrop for the hunt season's excitement.

The home, circa 1770, was Conyers Old Store in 1810, Finks' General Store in 1850 and a hippie commune in 1970. Its architecture is typical of old Virginia homes you can still find deeply buried in the country. You wonder if you're coming to nowhere when you leave Sperryville for an eight-mile jaunt down Route 231, a narrow, rural back road,

recently designated by the Commonwealth as a Scenic Byway, in the foothills of the Blue Ridge. The Conyers House thus becomes a destination in itself.

You pass an old brown barn and split rail fence, just before approaching the first entrance and seeing the small sign announcing Conyers House. Four levels high, the cafe-au-lait colored, clapboard house is dominated by the three-story porch on the front and porches on both sides.

Its growing popularity was causing the B&B to burst at the seams, so the Cartwright-Browns recently added a two story, 15-foot-square addition. They also put in three more private baths. The hunts pack in guests during the weekends, so calling in advance is important. Part of the recent expansion, the dining room accommodates more guests and has a fireplace at one end.

Dinner is by reservations only. Although guests dress informally, they often include the socially and politically prominent from Washington, D.C. The menu features such dishes as trout almondine, pork tenderloin and stuffed game hens. If you happen to visit on a weekend when the hunt leaves from The Conyers House, you'll see a stirrup cup, often Irish whiskey, offered to the field before the hunt goes out. After the hunt, the riders return to an immense hunt breakfast, a gastronomic sight to behold with the three stuffed pheasants as centerpiece, the signature of The Conyers House. Room rates regularly include an afternoon tea when you arrive and a hearty breakfast by the fire or out on the veranda.

The interiors are country cluttered, rustic and almost like a hunting lodge. You find mountings of African wildlife. The living room, formerly the country store dating from 1770, is dominated by books, large paintings, Hogarth etchings, Chinese rugs and a grand piano covered with silver framed family photos (past and present). The large formal dining room displays elegant silver service, and family heirlooms furnish the inn throughout, along with treasures collected during the owners' international travels. Hosts Norman and Sandra Cartwright-Brown speak French, Italian, German and some Arabic.

Rocking chairs are on the porches. And for the burned-out, work-oholic seeking R&R, weekdays are the perfect time to come for a quiet rock. The Hill House cottage, behind the Main House, and the Old Cellar Kitchen room allow pets.

Besides ride yourself, learn to ride or see the Rappahannock Hunt off, you can climb Old Rag Mountain, attend a half-day workshop on innkeeping from January through September, or venture into Warrenton, Charlottesville or Sperryville to search for antiques. Play or fish in the Hughes River. Fifteen minutes from the finest nouvelle cuisine on the east coast.

*Slate Mills Rd.*
*Sperryville, VA 22740*
*703/987-8025*

*Left at Sperryville Emporium, left on Rt. 522, right on Rt. 231. Drive eight miles, left on Rt. 707. One night's deposit required. Returnable less $20.*

# JORDAN HOLLOW FARM INN

*Swiss Postcard Setting*

"A horse, a horse, my kingdom for a horse!" raged the embattled King Richard III. Well, that's what you will find here, an equestrian delight.

Marley and Jetze Beers have restored a 200-year-old horse farm six miles south of Luray Caverns and Shenandoah National Park. It is located in what seems like a secluded, private valley one mountain range removed from the more familiar Shenandoah Valley of Virginia. It's like stumbling upon a quiet surprise untouched by time.

Stories abound about the Civil War. General Stonewall Jackson once marched along the edge of the property and over the New Market Gap. In the late 1930s the farm was converted into a nine-hole golf course and the farmhouse

was used as the clubhouse. Cleat marks can still be seen in the floors.

During World War II the club closed and the farm again became a horse farm. The Beers purchased the rundown place in 1979. It had finally deteriorated and become a pig farm. "What a mess!" Marley declares with vigor. Over time many horse breeds have been raised here: Tennessee Walkers, thoroughbreds, quarter horses, and most recently the Beers are raising German Holsteiner and Norwegian Fjord horses.

The farm stretches out for 45 acres. There is a fantastic view of the Blue Ridge Mountains everywhere you turn.

All of the farm buildings are original, except for Rowe's Lodge, the 16 bed-room lodge that blends in with the rest of the inn and houses all the guest

rooms. The lodge has private baths and one meeting room. What guests like most is the wrap-around sundeck, where they can sit for hours feasting on the incredible views.

The Beers, who have traveled the world for inn ideas, are wonderful hosts. They love to entertain their guests, share stories and challenge a chess or ping pong player. Marley is not only a "triple A" chef, but also an experienced horse rider and artist. Jetze speaks Dutch, German and "American" fluently.

They have simply but tastefully renovated Jordan Hollow into a modern, comfortable abode without losing any of its charm and serenity.

The four dining rooms are a cut above the ordinary. Two are the early log cabin rooms, a third is known as the

"Fox" room and the fourth is called the "African" room. During mild weather guests like to dine on the front veranda or out in the yard under the old maple trees.

Eating is a major part of the experience at Jordan Hollow. You might call the offerings eclectic; they are a blend of grandma's country cooking, some French cuisine and a dash of African and Middle Eastern seasonings.

Also on the grounds is the "Watering Trough Pub," a full service cocktail lounge with live entertainment available Friday and Saturday evenings. The building used to be a stable, and you can see the old beams left exposed during the renovation.

There are enough activities to keep you occupied so that you never need venture out of your cozy hollow until departure, if you so desire. Volleyball, hiking, cross country skiing in the winter months and a variety of indoor board games are among the offerings.

The horses make this colonial farm special. Guests may bring their own horses, but the Livery Ltd., the inn's stable, also offers a nice selection of English and western trail mounts. Scenic trail rides are matched to your level of skill at a rate of $15 per hour.

Nearby you can canoe, fish, cross country or downhill ski, golf, play tennis, attend an auction or visit museums, antique places and craft shops.

Amid this private, lush valley you can sightsee the Luray Caverns, Shenandoah National Park or George Washington National Forest. Through the mountain pass you can reach the New Market Battlefield and the Massanutten or Bryce ski areas. Staunton and Charlottesville are about an hour away.

Jordan Hollow not only caters to couples looking for a recreational getaway but also to the conference market. Meeting facilities have been professionally designed to serve groups of up to 30 people.

Why do conferees prefer this country cloister over some city hotel? "Work doesn't seem like work because you feel as though you are home! During breaks we can sit on the porch, walk around the meadow, ride a horse or even picnic on the spur of the moment," they reply.

*Rt. 2, Box 375*
*Stanley, VA 22851*
*703/778-2285 or 2209*

*Rt. 340 south of Luray; left onto Rt. 624. Left on Rt. 689. Right on Rt. 626; inn on right.*
*Reservations guaranteed by credit card or check for one night's stay. Cancellations must be made within one week* *prior to arrival date. Check-in 3 p.m.; check-out, 12 noon.*

# BELLE GRAE INN
*Rambling Victorian*

An authentically restored 1870 masterpiece, the 17-room inn caters to the traveling business person as well as tourists.

Innkeeper Michael Organ offers a full American breakfast (or if you desire, a continental breakfast with newspaper brought to your room), lunch and dinner. "We prepare fresh daily," he emphasizes with pride. All stops are pulled out for private parties or weekend dining, with the flair of live music and a spectrum of courses amid candlelight. Menus are posted daily.

The soup might be cream of asparagus; the appetizer, homemade pasta. Garden fresh salad with homemade poppy seed dressing is followed by choice of entrees: charcoaled swordfish, or tenderloin of beef covered with backfin crab in a bearnaise sauce. Vegetables might include bourbon car-

rots, fresh broccoli, or "twice-baked" potatoes. Rounding out the menu are homemade breads and desserts, including such specialties as Amaretto mousse with a macaroon cookie, chocolate peanut butter pie, white chocolate-macadamia nuts parfait with raspberry sauce, or smudge pie (graham cracker based with chocolate ice cream, crushed nut nougat filling, vanilla ice cream and hot fudge on top). All told, the food is superb.

Food operations are set up to handle bus tours of 40 with advance notice. Guests are seated within five minutes and 45 minutes later can be back on their way. The innkeepers have developed a reliable reputation for their expediency and attract much business from New Jersey and Pennsylvania.

Belle Grae's meeting facilities offer the business executive a place to get

away for a small group seminar. Accompanying spouses can easily walk to the downtown shopping district.

Tapping into the Baltimore-Washington-Richmond business world, the inn offers some rooms furnished for corporate clientele. The guest rooms in the annex feature desks; oversized baths called dressing rooms; phones; extra-firm, queensized beds; and color television.

When visiting Belle Grae, you may get no further than the veranda. The wicker rockers are mighty inviting! White gingerbread decorates the porch of the main, original building which is built of brick, a prevalent building material in Virginia. The ornate, double door entrance contains four striking stained glass panels in hues of purple and green. The inn's name is engraved inside a crystal oval.

You come into a foyer, with a mauve dining room to your left. You notice a stunning marble mantle. This room leads into another dining area, which emanates into the next section of the inn. This is the bistro, which goes to the outside courtyard.

To the right of the foyer is a lounge and formal sitting room. Adjoining is a small bedroom with private bath. Further down the foyer is the office area. Period reproductions, as well as antiques, are scattered throughout the inn. Somewhere along the line, "Bell Boy" will greet you with his boxer dog smile.

When you go upstairs to the other guest rooms, you see a lovely, stained glass scene in the alcove area. Many rooms have private baths and fireplaces. They are furnished nicely, all a little differently. One room has a trundle bed that folds down. And if you have never bathed in a Victorian, claw-footed tub, this will be your chance.

The bathrooms may be better-stocked than your own, with such amenities as English herb soap, shampoo, moisturizer, toothbrush and herb bath foam. You'll also find in your room a decanter of sherry with two long-stemmed glasses.

Southern hospitality is the rule here. You have access to chess and backgammon in the sitting room, television in the parlor, reading in any quiet corner and merry-making in the music rooms.

Atop a hill in Staunton's Historic Newtown District, Belle Grae is named after two mountains in view: Betsy Belle and Mary Grae. The Scotch-Irish, who settled the area because it reminded them of their homeland, named the mountains for landmarks in Scotland.

The mountain-valley scenery continues today to be the magnet of this Shenandoah Valley town. It is President Woodrow Wilson's birthplace and the home of the Statler brothers. Mary Baldwin College and Stuart Hall preparatory for girls are other focal points of the old, full-of-atmosphere hamlet of Staunton. A mammoth antique warehouse captivates many a visitor. Walking tours expose you to the local history.

*515 West Frederick St.*
*Staunton, VA 24401*
*703/886-5151*

*Exit 57 off I-81, onto Rt. 250 west into Staunton. Left on Frederick Street. Breakfast included in rate; lunch $5 -*

*$10; dinner $5 - $20. Reservations accepted with one night's deposit.*

# FREDERICK HOUSE
*Well-Executed Restoration*

Several years ago a native son renounced the pressurized lifestyle of the Washington, D. C., area to return home to Staunton, where he purchased a cluster of three rundown, ancestral homes and restored them to immaculate beauty.

Joe Harman, a former banker, and his wife Evy, who had pursued an insurance career, have worked wonders with three townhouses. What was once a downtown eyesore is now an inn complex resonant with Greek Revival charm and handsomeness.

The three buildings were built between 1810 and 1910. During the extensive renovation more than 175 tons of debris were removed! New everything has gone into Frederick House, from the roof on down to the plumbing, wiring,

heating, air-conditioning and security system.

Built in 1810, the Young House displays a Jeffersonian architecture closely akin to a home on the University of Virginia campus. Builders who had worked for Thomas Jefferson also built several homes elsewhere in Virginia. The Young House is probably one such home in the lower Shenandoah Valley. Joe's ancestors owned the Young House and the Womack House in 1895.

The Bowers House goes back to 1850. When her husband was killed in a train accident, Mrs. Bowers started a boarding house. She kept a cow in the backyard, where larkspur now blooms in the spring and summer against the outline of a nostalgic, white picket fence. The Harmans, who live in their inn, also

own a retail business and farm nearby.

They have furnished the inn with their personal collection of American antiques and paintings by Virginia artists. The interiors portray an elegant simplicity of old-world style. The appearance is scrupulously clean, the bathrooms modern, wallpaper and carpet smartly displayed. Greens, blues and mauves in soft muted tones set the color scheme. The curtains and bedspreads are all coordinated. Beds are over-sized for sleeping comfort, and each room has bathrobes laid out for the convenience of guests.

A common room goes off from the lobby and contains books and magazines. Some of the bedrooms have their own balcony or porch. Striking appointments include a lovely, curved staircase, some original dentil trim, a handmade fanlight in one gable and a one-story portico with balustrade.

A range of eating places nearby offers a good selection for lunch or dinner.

Frederick House sits in the midst of Staunton's walking tour. Your host can help you plan your sightseeing time. You are across from Mary Baldwin College and close to the Woodrow Wilson Birthplace, the Museum of American Frontier Culture, Statler Brothers Museum and Gypsy Hill Park. Right next door is an athletic club equipped with work-out and gym facilities, track, sauna, whirlpool and an indoor swimming pool. Within easy walking are enticing shops and antique stores. Staunton is one of the oldest cities west of the Blue Ridge Mountains.

You are convenient to the Blue Ridge Parkway, Skyline Drive, Lexington's Horse Center and lots of outdoor recreational pursuits from golfing and canoeing to fishing and horseback riding. The hilly city is three hours from Washington, D.C., or Williamsburg, and two hours from Richmond.

An Amtrak train station is only a couple of blocks away. Babysitting is available.

*P.O. Box 1387*
*Frederick and New Streets*
*Staunton, VA 24401*

*703/885-4220*
*Exit 57 off I-81, Rt. 250 west.*
*Reservations guaranteed by deposit or credit card. Cancellations 24 hours prior to 6 p.m. of arrival date.*

# THORNROSE HOUSE

*English Tradition*

Family owned and operated, Thornrose House bestows such TLC upon guests that you'll want to return again and again. Innkeepers Carolyn and Ray Hoaster patterned their establishment after a favorite B&B in Devon, England, and the couple, along with their two daughters, were drawn to Staunton because of its old-world charm and beautiful natural surroundings.

The Hoasters, originally from the Washington, D. C., area, became innkeepers (a dream of long-standing) following Ray's retirement from the Air Force. During several trips to England, they sampled over 50 bed and breakfasts and are well aware of the "creature comforts" that please their guests. They chose a modified Georgian home in

Staunton's Gypsy Hill area, Thornrose House, and have been receiving B&B guests since 1985.

Family heirlooms, German-American furniture and salvaged conversation pieces from old Staunton homes furnish the interior. Guests have free reign over the expansive entrance-way, dining room and sitting room, made especially pleasant with a fireplace and grand piano. Of special architectural note are the stairway and interior columns.

Each of the three guestrooms is air-conditioned and has a private bath en-suite. "Canterbury" offers a king-sized bed in rose surroundings. Lake-blue "Windermere" features a queen-sized bed, antique standing closet and early telephone case given second life as a

washstand. "Yorkshire" (in tribute to the "vet," James Herriot) is accented with English lace at the windows and has a double, four-poster bed. Footed tub enthusiasts will enjoy this bathroom.

Breakfast is an elaborate and lengthy affair. The house specialty, Bircher-muesli, is a Swiss cereal of oats, fruit, nuts and whipped cream, a secret recipe that Carolyn will share with anyone who asks! This is followed by a "buster" of a breakfast platter with bacon, sausage, eggs and toast. Special diets are happily catered to with advance notice. And, of course, in the true English tradition, afternoon tea is served — complete with Royal Albert china.

You will enjoy strolling across the street to the 300-acre Gypsy Hill Park to play golf, tennis (rackets and balls provided), swim or people-watch. Sometimes you may have to stop traffic, not so you can cross, but to allow "mama" duck and her ducklings to waddle to the park for swimming lessons. They nest under a shade tree in the Hoaster yard and enjoy the park, too, as they rendezvous with peacock, swan and deer friends there.

Back on the Thornrose House home front, you have a lovely yard to relax in. Landscaping focuses on pergolas (Greek Revival colonnades) entwined with bittersweet and wisteria. The wraparound veranda is reminiscent of another age — grab a rocker!

Your innkeepers, both musicians, are active in the music and theater circles of Staunton. They know the cultural offerings well and can help you plan your activities or provide directions to nearby fine dining. Staunton, the "Queen City of The Shenandoah Valley," is home to Mary Baldwin College, Woodrow Wilson's birthplace, the Statler Brothers (of country music fame) and the Museum of American Frontier Culture, one of Virginia's newest tourist attractions.

An extra-special event at Thornrose House is their "Victorian Sampler," a two-night, three-day adventure into the late 19th century. You'll enjoy good friends and experience the cuisine (care to try some "kedgeree"?), music and games of the Victorian era.

All in all, Thornrose House provides a berth for meeting new friends, or relaxing with old. In the words of Carolyn and Ray: "Our aim is to make your stay at Thornrose House the most memorable of your journey."  ♪

*531 Thornrose Ave.*
*Staunton, VA 24401*
*703/885-7026*

*I-64/I-81, Exit 57; follow Rt. 250 west,*
*left on Thornrose Ave.*

# ANDERSON COTTAGE

*Sweet Old Place*

What will impress you indelibly about this rambling old house is the fact that nothing has changed about it, for at least a century, you will think.

The owner and hostess, Jean Randolph Bruns, has been a journalist, real estate broker and world traveler. Perhaps this background combination conspired to give her an appreciation of the family homeplace as it was — so she had the good sense to leave it untouched for others to enjoy.

The original log portion of the house is visible in some of the rooms and once served as a tavern in the late 18th century. An entrance hall joins the two main structures. Over the years other rooms were added, which is why the house gives such a sprawling appearance.

Anderson Cottage once housed a girls' school. In the present owner's family for over a hundred years, the house has also been a private home, a summer inn and a vacation home.

Today it is serving bed and breakfast guests.

Four bedrooms, with two parlors, and spacious porches are open to guests. The rough, old plaster and crooked walls, built without the benefit of modern-day squaring techniques, and the old wooden floors lend an appealing charm. Nothing is superficially slick here. You are on a trip back in time, reminiscent of Europe's old world in some ways.

Because the house does not have central heat it closes November 1 and reopens in the spring. It is situated in a quiet, peaceful village in the Allegheny Mountains. You will enjoy easing back into a rocker just to listen to the birds sing or to catch up on some good reading from the cottage's bookshelves. The expansive, level yard is ideal for croquet and badminton.

The perpetually warm stream from the Warm Springs pools flows through the two-acre property. You can walk to the famous pools, which bubble up at

98° F. Neighboring Gristmill Square has an exceptional restaurant, and small shops dot the village.

On rainy days you can contentedly hole up in Anderson Cottage and play games or work jigsaw puzzles.

Sports facilities abound in this Bath County resort area. Your choices cover the Cascades and Lower Cascades Golf Courses, horseback riding at The Homestead, fishing at the Homestead or in local streams, swimming at Lake Moomaw or Douthat Park, walking the prolific trails and driving the scenic backroads.

Garth Newel concerts every Sunday afternoon and many Saturday afternoons from July through September give you chamber music of high quality. Further north in Monterey is the Highland Maple Festival in the early spring and the Highland County Fair in August. The historic town of Lexington is an hour's drive away. You may also wish to visit the Cass Scenic Railroad over the line in West Virginia.

Your hostess serves a full country breakfast. The dining room is in the log part of the home. An open fire takes the chill off the cool, mountain air. It's easy to remember Grandma's home.

*Box 176*
*Warm Springs, VA 24484*
*703/839-2975*

*4 hours from Washington, D.C. From Staunton, Rt. 254 west, merge into Rt. 42 west. Take Rt. 39 west to Warm Springs, left on Rt. 692, fourth house on left.*

*Deposit required to confirm reservations; returned with adequate notice.*

# MEADOW LANE LODGE

*Paradise*

You just know you've come to a special vacation spot as you wind your way up a narrow road between meadows and woods. You can't see the estate from the road; you have to penetrate deep into the property. As you emerge into a large clearing, you finally see a three-part, white frame house with green and yellow trim — the main lodge. All so tidy and immaculate. And very inviting.

Around a curve in front of Meadow Lane Lodge are two smaller buildings. One used to be an old dairy house. The other was the ice house; in bygone days ice was cut on the river and stored here. Now they are an office and a storage building. Further back is a converted building with antique cars on the ground floor. Overhead is a hotel suite, furnished in a contemporary style with beamed ceilings.

Out back a barn stables horses and donkeys. Guests may bring their horses to board — horse trails thread all through the Allegheny mountains and valleys. The George Washington National Forest roads add to the extensive network of riding trails.

Beyond the barn lies an area called the deck, an overlook built on a platform. This is a favorite spot of guests. From this post they can observe a nature preserve, where wild animals come to feed and drink. Deer, fox, blue heron and all sorts of other birds, beavers along the marshes, ad infinitum. If it's indigenous to Virginia, you'll find it here — flora and fauna.

The 1600-acre expanse of land is awesome. It gives the outdoor enthusiast options galore. Hiking trails are marked. In spring you forage through thickets of redbud, dogwood and wildflowers. Summer gives way to rhododendron and laurel. The fall foliage creates spectacular beauty in this mountainous region.

Croquet is the house specialty. Meadow Lane belongs to the United States Croquet Association and draws the serious player. A dynaturf tennis court is available to guests, but the adjacent swimming pool is private, so you need to obtain permission from the innkeepers, Catherine and Philip Hirsh.

The Hirsh family has owned Meadow Lane for three generations. It was part of the original land grant from

*Continued next page*

## Meadow Lane Lodge, Continued

King George III of England to Charles Lewis, one of Virginia's early settlers.

The foundation of an old log cabin, circa 1750, is visible from the early 19th-century slave cabin on the west side of the Jackson River. A stockade was built around the cabin during the French and Indian War and eventually became known as Fort Dinwiddie. George Washington may have slept here! At least he made his rounds here. The barns date from the 1920s when Meadow Lane was a horse breeding farm.

Two miles of the pristine Jackson River flow through the property. Meadow Lane's water supply originates from a limestone spring one and a half miles up river.

Twice a year the Hirshes stock the Jackson with brown trout. The best trout fishing occurs in the spring. The unpolluted stream delivers small mouth bass, rock bass, blue gills, pickerel and fall fish. There's a good ole swimming hole in the river opposite the field barn; a canoe also awaits your pleasure.

Catherine's hobbies are gardening and raising animals, evident everywhere. Jack Russell terriers Ruff and Jaws roam free. Nubian goats and sheep graze the secluded, lush meadows. You occasionally hear a bray out of Harvey, a white donkey who is spoiled. There is the half-breed cat, part domestic and part bob. Peacocks strut around, sometimes dropping their spectacular plumage. The pet duck is the only animal allowed in the swimming pool. Japanese Silkies, a type of chicken with black skin and white feathers, lend an air of sophistication to the melange.

Guests stay an average of four days here. Much to do for the venturesome; unsurpassed opportunities to dawdle for the lazy.

The lodge is as well kept as its manicured grounds. Rooms spotless, simply but tastefully decorated in a combination of modern comfort and antique splendor. Two stone fireplaces set off the gracious living room. Lodging runs the gamut: doubles, suites with fireplaces, and private cottages (one is actually in town overlooking the hillside).

In the morning the Hirshes serve a full southern breakfast in a lovely, long dining room. Lots of windows give it a cheerful, country atmosphere. If the batter bread — an old tradition in Virginia — makes you salivate, the innkeepers don't mind giving out their recipe.

You can eat your other meals at excellent restaurants nearby. There is shopping, and you won't want to miss the Bacova Guild showroom. Bacova gift items, recognized nationally for their distinctiveness, are made in this wilderness! The Garth Newel Music Center hosts concerts during the summer months and in October — a real unexpected treat. Golf is minutes away at the famed Cascades of The Homestead Resort. Lake Moomaw, a man-made lake, offers boat launching, beach swimming, and more recreation. Virginia's "little Switzerland," Monterey, is a short drive north. You can drive east to visit historic Lexington or in an hour to the world class Greenbrier Hotel in West Virginia.

*Meadow Lane Lodge*
*Star Route A, Box 110*
*703/839-5959*

*Warm Springs, VA 24484*
*Rt. 39 west, 4 miles west of Rt. 220.*
*Open April-December.*

*Deposits due 10 days before reservation*
*date. Refundable if cancelled 7 days*
*prior to arrival. Check-in 2 p.m.; check-*
*out 12 noon. $18 per rod, per day for*
*fishing.*

# INN AT GRISTMILL SQUARE

*Allegheny Valley Delight*

If you have never been one valley over from the Shenandoah Valley, then you are in for a surprising quintessential treat when you wind your way over the Allegheny Mountains to Gristmill Square. There you'll find one of the nation's few surviving mills, which has been in continuous operation since 1771.

Hosts Janice McWilliams and her son Bruce will make you feel right at home. The bucolic town setting and environs whisper shades of Vermont. And that might be why the McWilliams, professional innkeepers, left the Green Mountain State to take over this warmer climate hideaway.

Five 19th century buildings cluster around a courtyard. The restaurant, built of red siding, reminds you of a barn. You know the reason for the Gristmill Square name when you see the waterwheel along one side. The current mill was built in 1900 and is fed by Warm Spring Run. Inside, the Simon Kenton Pub teems with ambience. A few steps below is a graveled-floor wine cellar, where guests, in lieu of a list, can personally select their wine. An array of glasses atop a chopping block spells tasting time. The large cogs and gears of the gristmill are in plain view.

The Waterwheel Restaurant's food and service reign supreme. There are different menus for summer and winter, with daily specials. Fresh local trout and fettucine alla Carbonara (Virginia ham) will more than satisfy your appetite.

Also in the square are the small country stores (formerly the blacksmith shop) on separate levels with antiques, crafts and deli items. The old miller house and hardware store now house eight guest rooms, including quarters called the Tower Apartment.

Across the lane is the Steel House, a restored private home with four guest rooms. Behind that are a pool and tennis courts. The rooms and suites, decorated differently, display antiques, old prints, country and contemporary moods. A continental breakfast is brought to your room each morning. And there is a refrigerator in each room for your convenience.

The inn borders the Hot Springs resort area of The Homestead, whose world-famous Cascades golf courses are 20 minutes away. Besides all the activities synonymous with a resort area, including Homestead skiing in the winter, Warm Springs is in the middle of trout fishing country. Most any time of the year you'll find fly fishermen casting into the Cascades Stream (considered one of the finest in the Eastern United States), Jackson River and other local streams. From the inn you can walk to the historic Warm Springs Pools, where thermal waters 98°F gush out of the ground 1,200 gallons per minute. Men and women have separate quarters, of course, as 18th century etiquette dictated. Thomas Jefferson may have designed the two circular bath houses, site of a health spa since Indian times.

Gristmill Square's romantic aura entices many a couple to make a getaway for a few days to enjoy the Alleghenies' magnificent outdoors. You can comb the many byways of America, but you won't find a more pleasurable playground than the area served by Gristmill Square.

*P.O . Box 359*
*Warm Springs, VA 24484*
*703/839-2231*

*Near the intersection of Rts. 220 and 39 on Rt. 645.*
*Deposit required, refunded up to 7 days*
*in advance or, otherwise, if inn rents cancelled space. Check-in 2 p.m.; check-out 12 noon.*

# CALEDONIA FARM
*In the Virginia Foothills*

Splendor for all seasons! An overnight stay anytime, in the stone home at Caledonia Farm will convince you of that. The quiet sounds of nature and country living are gentle on the nerves! You would be hard pressed to find a more beautiful setting. To watch the sun set behind the Blue Ridge Mountains to the west is one incomparable show after another.

Caledonia took well over five years to build and was completed in 1812 by the Dearings, who lived there until 1916. The house was rented until 1948 and then fell upon hard times. It was inhabited by pigs and chickens before William Pullen rescued the property in 1963, introduced water and electricity

and restored it to house-tour quality in 1965.

International broadcaster Phil Irwin bought it in 1967 and made it a B & B in 1985. He had hosted the "Breakfast Show" on Voice of America for nearly 24 years, but entertains now on a much reduced scale. He speaks some German and Danish and has traveled to 49 countries, 50 states and all but one of the Canadian provinces. He's personally visited B & B's all over North America to glean ideas for Caledonia. His wife, Florence, is president and founder of a Washington-based consulting firm specializing in technical training and research for the federal government. She commutes about an hour away when

traffic is light. They visit other B & B's to "get away."

Caledonia sits back from the road. Maple trees and firs surround the home. Persimmon, black walnut, oak and dogwood also dot the landscape. A breezeway connects the manor house to the original summer kitchen, now the great cottage. Splitrail and stone fences traverse the rolling countryside, peppered with grazing Angus and occasional deer, black bear and other wildlife. Apple trees separate the house from the barn and machinery sheds. You enter the Federal style home through a new matching wing, where the kitchen and dining room are now. The house is furnished appropriately.

Wrought-iron handles and thumb latches adorn all of the primitive looking doors, while antiques and a stone fireplace with the original carved mantle formalize the living room.

All the rooms feature newly exposed beamed ceilings. The two bedrooms in the main house each have a double bed, working fireplace, individual heat controls, air-conditioning, semi-private bath and those special mountain views.

On the ground level, early American kitchen utensils hang over the large, stone fireplace in Caledonia's winter kitchen along with a Pennsylvania-Kentucky rifle used in the Revolutionary War. The rifle belonged to Captain John Dearing, and one of his heirs returned it when the family home was restored. Phil also promised the rifle would always remain with the house.

Across the new breezeway is the old summer kitchen where the cooking fireplace of 1807 burns again today in the living room. Upstairs, where the house servants were quartered, is the bedroom and full modern bath...the equivalent of a two-and-a-half-room suite.

At hourly intervals, Phil serves breakfast from a menu including eggs Benedict, omelets, smoked salmon, grits and freshly ground coffee. During an evening social hour, he treats guests to his special hors d'oeuvres. History buffs will soak up his book, recording the history of the home and family. Outdoor lovers will appreciate gallivanting around the working farm or hay riding in Phil's old pickup to a picturesque clearing by a stream in the Shenandoah National Park. Three porches offer a variety of scenic vistas.

You are only five miles away from the award-winning Oasis Vineyard. The farm looks up at the Skyline Drive. Trails through the Shenandoah National Park take you to waterfalls and mountaintops. Phil has all the maps and information. Cross-country skiers: you're in paradise. Spelunkers: you're in the center of cave country. Civil War aficionados: you're an hour and a half from 90 percent of the major battlefields.

*Rt. 1, Box 2080*
*Flint Hill, VA 22627*
*703/675-3693*

*Four miles north of Washington, Va, on Rt. 628.*
*Reservations confirmed with first night deposit or by Mastercard or Visa, refundable, less 20 percent for cancella-* *tions 48 hours in advance. $30 for weeknight, candlelight dinner by advance reservation. $5 bag lunch. Extended visit rates.*

# FOSTER-HARRIS HOUSE
*Friendly and Gracious*

Not to be confused with Washington, D.C., the tiny community of Washington, Va., boasts a population of 250 citizens. Named for its surveyor, George Washington, the town has the *first* Washington Museum, which you will want to explore. The Foster-Harris House is located on the edge of town.

Patrick Foster and Camille Harris operate the B&B, a Victorian house, circa 1900. They bought the home in 1981 and spent the next three years getting it into shape. The couple lives in the downstairs portion of the house with their two daughters and will charm you with their friendliness.

Upstairs the two guest rooms share a bath and sitting room. The suite includes a private bath, sitting room, bedroom and kitchen. You will find fresh flowers everywhere.

Pat, a renovation specialist and decorative painter, has preserved the Victorian character of the home. He is skilled in faux bois, a favorite painting technique George Washington admired and that traces its roots centuries ago to Italy. You will see Pat's decorative touches throughout the home. They are false finishes that fool the eye, painted effects that look real, like the "marble" in the bathroom and the "cherry" chair rail. This art form disappeared during the Industrial Age but in recent years has experienced a resurgence.

From an overflowing garden, Camille started a floral business on the side, providing the only such service in rural Rappahannock County. She also prepares the full continental breakfast that comes with your lodging and includes freshly-baked goods, coffee, tea, fruit and juice.

Some of the antiques in the Foster-Harris House are for sale. Ask your hosts for the listing. You'll find that one of the inn's greatest pleasures is relaxing on the porch swing and viewing the foothills of the Blue Ridge.

Local restaurants offer casual fare to fine dining. You are a half-hour's drive from Culpeper, Front Royal, Warrenton and Luray.

Good antique shopping is to be had in Rappahannock County and five minutes from the inn in Sperryville. There is no limit to the pastimes of this area: fishing, hiking, horseback riding, attending auctions, visiting Luray Caverns, swimming, sightseeing the vineyards, going to country fairs and cruising the Skyline Drive, 10 minutes from Washington.

*P.O. Box 333*
*Washington, VA 22747*
*703/675-3757*

*From Warrenton take Rt. 211 for 25 miles. Turn right at first entrance to Washington. Turn left at stop sign, go to last house in row, on right. From Sperryville take Rt. 211 east 6 miles; turn left at four-lane highway. Go almost a mile; first house on left after entering town.*
*Reservations suggested. Full payment in advance, 48-hour cancellation notice (refund less $10).*

# G AY STREET
*Morningside of the Blue Ridge*

Rappahannock County, like so many counties in the Commonwealth of Virginia, is chock full of history. Of singular note is the little town of Washington, the first Washington of them all. An hour west of the nation's capital, it predates George Washington's presidency and is the only town he named for himself after surveying it in 1746. The young surveyor laid out many communities, especially in the Shenandoah Valley.

Nestled quietly in one corner of this tiny hamlet, located on the morningside of the Blue Ridge Mountains, is the Gay Street Inn.

It too ensconces history — roughly 100 years of it. Your hosts, Donna and Robin Kevis, love to talk about it and the historic district of which it is a part. They themselves are new on the scene — having just come from Nantucket Island, Massachusetts, in August of 1987.

Carpenter Robin pursues hobbies of

fishing, collecting old cars and, you guessed it, fixing up old houses. Donna, a retired secretary, is a gourmet chef who, like her husband, enjoys taking the mystery out of old homes. The real rulers of their kingdom, however, are two house pets, a 14-year-old female Chesapeake Bay Retriever named Gimbal and a three-year-old Maine Coon cat, Kitty.

The inn has large, airy rooms with high ceilings. It is decorated with paper from the Shelbourne Museum Collection in Vermont. Exuding a Colonial atmosphere, the house brims with antique beds and side pieces. Guests can choose from among three comfortable rooms. They have for enjoyment a fireplace, as well as a tremendous view of the Blue Ridge Mountains and its lush meadows.

Hiking the rolling countryside, the Shenandoah National Park and the nearby Skyline Drive trails are a supreme treat.

You can also take a leisurely stroll to

the local shops and restaurants. Gay Street does serve a continental buffet breakfast, which features muffins as the house specialty. Donna makes all her own breads, fruit butters and preserves. Fresh fruit compote, juices, tea and coffee are served on nice settings of china and linens. Set-ups and nibbles are provided at cocktail hours.

If you make prior arrangements, your innkeepers can accommodate pets and children. They look forward to their guests and enjoy meeting the diverse people that come their way. They travel quite a bit themselves.

*P.O. Box 237*
*Washington, VA 22747*
*703/675-3288*

*From D.C. take I-66 west. At Gainesville/Warrenton Exit, take Rt. 29 to Warrenton, then Rt. 211 west to Washington, VA. 1 1/2 hrs. from D.C.*

# HERITAGE HOUSE
*American Country Pleasures*

This delightful 1837 manor house lies in the heart of historic Washington, Virginia — which is in the piedmont region of the state, not to be confused with the nation's capital an hour or two away. Built as a wedding home for his bride-to-be by Henry Johnson, the grandson of a freed Welsh bondsman, the house has grown from a simple two-over-two frame structure to a large town home with added rooms and enclosed porches.

From its picturesque white columns to the quaint pump room, original slaves' kitchen and the ice house in the side yard, you are surrounded by the heritage of days gone by.

Owners Nancy and Jim Thomasson have decorated each of the guest rooms with antiques, folk art and American handcrafts from Country Heritage, Nan's shop across the street that features the work of 130 professional American handcrafters.

Repeat bed and breakfast guests are often surprised to find that their room looks entirely different from their last stay. That's because if guests like the antique bed they slept on or the quilt over it, they can purchase it to take home!

Heritage House has three guest rooms and a large suite, which includes a bedroom, solarium, kitchen and

private bath. Guests are invited to make themselves at home in the living room and downstairs solarium. From books on log cabins and "country" collecting to Nan's spinning wheels and Jim's unusual oil can collection, there's plenty to capture your imagination. On arrival you are treated to tea and sweets.

The next morning you will find yourself lingering over the breakfast table, with its spread of fresh-baked breads and delicious egg casserole. As captivating as the food is the lively table conversation. Your host Jim is a theology professor at Georgetown University. He is also writing an historical novel based on the life of Soren Kierkegaard.

Your hostess Nan, when she is not in her shop or kitchen, directs crafters, quilts for the shop and serves on the town council.

The couple — "supervised" by a small herd of donkeys — is using 18th century hand tools to build a home on their "very" country property.

If you don't get to finish the stimulating table talk, you can make arrangements with the Thomassons for one of their colonial country suppers. Jim is also good for an impromptu walking tour at night around the historic village. He spices his discourse with colorful tidbits of history and entertaining tales.

How do Nan and Jim see their artful enterprise? "For us," Nan explains, "it's less like work and more like entertaining friends. We want others to come share with us the pleasures of American country life!" This is one B&B where — during weekdays — you can bring your young children.

While at Heritage House you will certainly want to step across the street to look for that perfect country accent to take back home. At Country Heritage you will find an extensive selection of symbols and moods that make up the distinctively country culture. The shop's philosophy is to preserve yesterday's crafts for tomorrow's generations. The Christmas display opens the first of every November, but all year round the shop carries pottery, quilts, dried flowers, folk art, unusual kitchen accessories, folk toys and lots of original designs.

Fishing, hiking, horseback riding, tennis, the Skyline Drive, other antique and craft shops, and a world-renowned, five-star restaurant are convenient diversions for you during your stay at Heritage House, in the foothills of the Blue Ridge Mountains.

This down-home comfort is 67 miles from Washington, D.C.; 110 from Richmond; 60 from Charlottesville; 13 from the entrance to the Skyline Drive; and a mere 1430 miles from Crookston, Minnesota and Lake Wobegon (a personal interest of this book's author because her sister married into Garrison Keillor's family and a special interest of your innkeepers because they love that spell-binding tale weaver).  ⁊

*Main St.,*
*P.O. Box 90*
*Washington, Va 22747*
*703/675-3207, 3738*

*On Rt. 211, 22 miles west of Warrenton, 5 miles east of Sperryville. Up to 48 hours, 10% cancellation fee charged;* *within 48 hours, 20%; balance refunded if no one turned away. Children welcomed during weekdays.*

# SYCAMORE HILL HOUSE
*High Ranking Scenery*

Somewhat off the beaten path, because it rests atop Menefee Mountain 1,043 feet high, Sycamore Hill House and Gardens is one of the few contemporary-styled B&B's. It was planned that way to take full advantage of the overwhelming mountain view.

Built from Virginia fieldstone, the secluded home sits on 52 wooded acres near historic Washington, Virginia. You are just minutes from the Skyline Drive.

The most prominent feature of the Blue Ridge Mountain home is its 75-foot semicircular veranda and patio. You can sit indoors or out and enjoy the panoramic view of the undisturbed countryside and engulfing mountains.

Looking out over the waves of mountains is a real feast. The foreground is a colorful design all its own — dozens of annual and perennial flower beds that more than please the eye.

Your hosts are Kerri and Stephen Wagner. A former registered lobbyist, Kerri worked for 15 years on Capitol Hill with agricultural concerns. She has retired from that life to handle full time the operations of her B&B. Her oriental needlework is displayed throughout the house. Gardening is another specialty, and her colorful orchids, African violets, other flowers, plants and trees beautify tabletops and corners.

Steve, a free-lance illustrator, has had his art published nationally and in

Europe. He is currently working on a series of projects for Time-Life Books. Other clients include such giants as the National Geographic, the U.S. Information Agency, the Washington Post, New Republic, and U.S. News and World Report. He focuses his personal art on wildlife and nature, and often photographs birds, animals and flowers. One of his photographs of a McKenna's Giant Columbine was used as the model for Sycamore's logo. You will see many of the original paintings of his published pieces hanging in the B&B.

A newcomer to the bed and breakfast scene, Sycamore Hill limits accommodations to ensure the comfort and privacy of guests. The Peach Suite consists of a large bedroom with a queen bed, private bath with tub and shower, and a sitting room. Beautiful hardwood floors peek out from under oriental rugs. A window seat with a small library looks out to a view of the woods. The setup is perfect for a weekend getaway.

The Blue Suite has a full kitchen, large living/dining room with queen bed, a complete bath. Ideal for longer retreats, the suite can accommodate four. There is new wall-to-wall carpeting, and the suite is amply stocked with books, games and plants. You have your own patio and picture windows from which to enjoy the sweeping tiers of mountain scenery.

Spring is a special time of the year at Sycamore. The dogwood and redbud are in bloom. In the Blue Suite you can literally wake up on a spring morning, see the sun rise over the pastures and mountains, and iris blooming almost at the foot of your bed. The fall, of course, gets painted like an artist's palette.

Your hostess offers you fresh baked goods upon arrival, plus coffee, beer, wine or a beverage of your choice. Evening mints and brandy or cognac are available in the suites. Elegant dinners are prepared for guests by advance reservation. The menu includes wine, appetizer or salad, entree with appropriate accompaniments, bread and dessert. You may select from a long entree list such delicacies as fresh fish, crab imperial, boneless chicken breast sauteed with lemon, fettucine alfredo, veal scallopine Marsala, stuffed pork chops, or down-home fare like chicken and dumplings.

Breakfast comes with your lodging and is also gourmet: omelets, spinach souffle with baked eggs, blueberry pancakes, sticky buns, baked apples and stuffed pears.

When you are not eating or relaxing with the view, you might want to hike the forest and meadows. You are bound to come upon deer, wild turkey, grouse, foxes, rabbits, or, at the very least, some delightful song birds.

Nearby options also include tennis, canoeing, horseback riding, antiquing, vineyard touring and exploring the Luray and Skyline caverns. You are 66 miles from Washington, D.C. 🖊

*Rt. 1, Box 978*
*Washington, VA 22747*
*703/675-3046*

*1 mile east of Washington, VA, at intersection of Rt. 683 and Rt. 211. Night's deposit confirms reservations;* *refunded less $20 if cancellation made 3 days prior to arrival and room is re-rented.*

# L'AUBERGE PROVENCALE

*Vous Souhaite la Bienvenue*

The innkeepers of L'Auberge Provencale invite you to discover what an inn South of France is like. You don't need to cross the ocean; simply come to White Post, a tiny rural community west of the Shenandoah River and the Blue Ridge, not far from Winchester.

White Post was first surveyed by George Washington in 1748. The young surveyor drove a white post in the ground to mark the route to the wilderness manor of Lord Thomas Fairfax. The home is gone but the white post remains, as do neighboring residences still in the English country-manor style.

L'Auberge Provencale is a striking limestone farmhouse built in 1753. Hessian soldiers did the woodworking, including the porch. Known as Mount

Airy, the large, center hall, federal style home has been restored, but all the floors are original. The main house has three dining rooms and two guest rooms with fireplaces. There are Victorian additions, but the octagonal dining room, created by seven French doors, has a modern air. One of the other dining rooms is decorated in Wedgwood blues with wide mouldings and a mantel trimmed in white.

A fourth-generation French chef purchased the property in 1981 with his wife. They added a four-bedroom guest house to what once was an 800-acre plantation at the time of Washington's surveying.

Decorated in an attractive Victorian manner, the six guest rooms have private baths, period antiques, oriental carpeting and French graphics. You can choose a high four-poster or iron bed, with such elegant amenities as eyelet pillowcases and embroidered towels. You are treated to sherry and fruited chocolate. Room service is available, if you so desire it.

The high point of your experience here is perhaps breakfast. Served on the porch or inside, it encompasses freshly squeezed orange juice, peaches and wild raspberries in champagne, eggs perfectly poached in veal stock with shallots and sprigs of tarragon — served atop ripe tomato slices, some non-ordinary cottage fries, cafe au lait, and homemade croissants and jams. Some food critics have pronounced the food preparation here to be among the best anywhere in the mid-Atlantic states.

The gourmet breakfast comes with lodging. Dinner is extra, but of equal caliber. The master chef uses fresh herbs, spices and vegetables from his own garden, as well as from some local farmers. The intricate recipes are a far cry from what passes as "French" in many sophisticated restaurants of large cities. You do not want to miss out on the meals when you visit L'Auberge Provencale. Not only will they score high to the palate, they surpass any food picture you'll ever see.

But don't let the dignity of the stone inn and its superb food fool you. You are in the country. You become fully aware of that when you wake up in the morning and see cows grazing in the adjoining pasture. The countryside is at your beck and call. There are several places to go horseback riding nearby. Country roads will take you to little villages such as Berryville and Stephens City, or to the Appalachian Trail crisscrossing the Blue Ridge Mountains. It's fairly easy to come upon deer, wild turkeys and other wildlife. The Skyline Drive begins a few miles from the inn.

Country auctions are held regularly and often reveal some irresistible antique bargains. You may wish to visit Blandy Farm, or quietly wile away the day on the porch.

*White Post, VA 22663*
*703/837-1375*

*70 miles from Washington, D.C. Travel west on Rt. 50; left onto Rt. 340. Inn is nearby on right. Dining rooms open Wed.-Sat., 6-10:30 p.m.; Sunday dinner, 4-9 p.m. Inn closed Mon. and* *Tues. Check-in 2 p.m.; check-out 11 a.m. Call 10 a.m.-10 p.m. for reservations. $50 deposit; four-day notice for refund.*

# BENSONHOUSE OF WILLIAMSBURG

*Sheldon's   Ordinary*

No matter how many times you have already been to Williamsburg, a night of bed and breakfast in this magnificent home is sufficient cause to bring you back to the cradle of America. Sheldon's Ordinary stands on its own merits. Its lovely peaceful setting is what dreams are made of.

The artistically landscaped grounds take advantage of the wooded setting atop a quiet hill. Enormous trees dwarf the flowering dogwoods and boxwoods. Along with the azaleas and masses of bulbs, they make springtime extra special. Periwinkle trails along the outer perimeters.

But the landscape design was not the only reason that Sheldon's Ordinary was on Virginia's 1986 garden tour. The home itself is architecturally significant. Beautifully proportioned, it was built in 1983 as an exact replica of the 18th century Sheldon's Tavern in Litchfield, Connecticut. Sheldon's Ordinary offers all the character and dignity of a classic, but with the newness and creature comforts of a modern dwelling.

From the outside you notice the large palladian window on the second floor. Inside you view hand-painted tiles of flowers and birds from the Caribbean – they adorn the facing of the living room fireplace mantel. Wide plank floors are made of antique heart of pine from Philadelphia. The family room is lined with oak paneling from an old church in Indiana, where your hosts are originally from. Antiques and reproductions fill the home, which is decorated in the style of Colonial Williamsburg.

The interior floor plan was specifically designed for gracious entertaining. On the third floor, guest rooms offer complete privacy. The queen-size bedroom features a fireplace, phone and television with cable. It overlooks a boxwood garden below and adjoins a bedroom with twin beds. The bath has separate entrances from both rooms. Unlike many B&B's a port-a-crib is available. There is also a queen-size sleep sofa in the guest area.

Your hosts are a physician who has a private practice and his wife. They are both involved in community affairs and love to share their favorite Willliamsburg sites with guests. In the winter they enjoy skiing with their younger children, and in the summer the family goes for the beach. Tricksie, their resident dog, will probably be the first to greet you at the front door.

When you arrive you are served hot or cold refreshments. With your lodging comes breakfast. Juice, fresh fruit, cereal, and homemade ham rolls and applesauce cake are served with coffee or tea in the dining room. Eggs are available on request.

Williamsburg, of course, is best known for the colonial restoration village, and is perhaps one of America's top tourist attractions. Some new buildings have been added, so if you haven't been to Colonial Williamsburg for a while, you will be in for a surprise. Sheldon's Ordinary is only three-quarters of a mile away. Other key attractions in the area include Busch Gardens, Jamestown and Yorktown. Belle Grove Plantation and Williamsburg Pottery are outstanding places you can add to a list of more things to see than you originally planned for.

Your hosts provide bicycles, which you may find to be a wonderful way to scoot around town. The College of William and Mary borders Colonial Williamsburg and is a natural spot for bike touring.

Bensonhouse offers additional rooms in other private homes and inns within three miles of Williamsburg.　✍

*c/o RSO*
*Bensonhouse of Williamsburg*
*2036 Monument Ave.*
*Richmond, VA 23220*
*804/648-7560*
*Call 10-6, M-F.*
*One hour from Richmond; 2 1/2 hours from Washington, D.C. Driving directions given at confirmation time. Reservations allow 10-day cancellation notice; deposit returned less $20 service charge.*

# A WILLIAMSBURG LEGACY

*Eighteenth Century Virginia*

Two major reasons usually draw the traveler to Williamsburg -- Historic Williamsburg and the College of William and Mary. A Williamsburg Legacy is ideally located for visiting either.

It is situated on the historic Jamestown Road, which has been traveled since the 1600s by the footsteps of the early settlers, the Revolutionary War militia, the prospering plantation farmers in their horse and carriages — down through America's pages of history to today's motorists.

The B&B is right across the street from the College of William and Mary, the nation's second oldest college. Parents and friends of current students, as well as prospective students on a college inspection tour, will find the quarters very convenient.

You are an easy 10-minute walk to the historic area of Williamsburg. In peak seasons you are often better off than the motorist trying to jockey for a parking place at the Visitors Center. Historic Williamsburg has added to its complex recently, so if you haven't been to the restored city in a while, there are new things to see. The DeWitt Wallace Decorative Arts Gallery and the reproduction of the nation's first mental institution round out the historic village. They are exceptional collections of early Americana, with an angle on the unusual.

Your hosts can tell you all about the goings on in the area. Their home is an eighteenth century design with handsome pine flooring. Each room comes alive with authentic furnishings of the Federal period. Every room in the house

can be reached from a center hall, which lends privacy to guests.

You wake up in the mornings in your canopy Pencil-post bed to the smells of the homebaked breads and muffins for your breakfast. The B&B serves a full breakfast to guests as part of the lodging arrangement.

Ed and Mary Ann Lucas, your hosts, came to Williamsburg to further their knowledge in American Federal period furnishings. They fell in love with the region so rich in American history and decided to live there.

Their side antique business, Painted Legacy, reflects their vast knowledge of 18th century antiques. The Lucases are avid dealers and collectors of fine antique furnishings, so you can add one more reason for coming to this part of Virginia. You may find that long-sought-for piece to fit your own decor at home. Ed and Mary Ann are a goldmine of information and love to converse with fellow antique buffs.

Their welcome mat is out for guests on a vacation or simply a weekend visit. They will treat you royally, from a bowl of fruit in your room to bath robes for lounging. The robe idea serves guests well — it is one less thing to pack and leaves your suitcase with room for higher priority items.

A Williamsburg Legacy offers three guest rooms. One features a suite with a fireplace. The interiors, of course, remind you of Colonial Williamsburg, with a simple, neat look.

If you exhaust the possibilities in town, you will find a fun-filled day at Busch Gardens. Other points of interest to take in are Water Country, Jamestown and Yorktown that form the historic triangle with Williamsburg, Williamsburg Pottery (which can easily be another full day's experience), the fine

old James River plantations, and, to get in a day at the ocean, Virginia Beach.

Williamsburg is 45 minutes from Richmond or Norfolk. It lies two and a half hours south of Washington, D.C. ⌐

*930 Jamestown Rd.*
*Williamsburg, VA 23185*
*804/220-0524*

*Off I-64. Credit card guarantee or one night's deposit by check. 4-day cancellation notice.*

# TRILLIUM HOUSE
*On the Blue Ridge*

In a Blue Ridge Mountain resort, Trillium House is as legitimate as they come. And to top that off, it is family owned and operated, so you really sink into comfortable feelings of home.

You travel a delightful country road to get there and might think you have arrived at an old homestead. Actually, it was built in 1983. The two-story, up-scale country inn is made of grayed cedar on the exterior. You enter through double doors right into the great room.

A free standing, woodburning stove warmly greets you. Antiques and an oriental rug add a highbrow touch. Above the great room you'll notice a half loft, loaded with books, leather chairs and maps — creating a most delightful library.

A dining room table and more informal seating are arranged on the other side of the fireplace. Guests have free use of a large TV, equipped with cable and VCR. Off to the side is an enclosed garden-type room, where guests like to gather to play cards and other games. Another free standing, woodburning stove lends a cozy mood. Large sliding glass windows yield a nice view of the outdoors. Fans are everywhere. A large arched window over the country-primitive porch outside is a telltale sign of the cathedral ceilings inside.

Guests have their pick of 10 rooms on the first or second floor. Some are twin, some queen. There are two suites. All have private baths and are soundproofed.

Family hosts Betty and Ed Dinwiddie

have decorated their bedrooms all with different personalities ranging from old world to contemporary. The rooms shine with cleanliness and order. Amenities abound – soap, shampoo, conditioners.

Shutters hang from most of the bedroom windows. For modern day comfort you can control heating and cooling to suit your individual liking in your room. And you get to sleep under handmade quilts and comforters.

The walls have lots of pictures, especially of the inn's namesake — trillium, a three-petal wildflower typically found in Virginia's mountains. Family heirlooms furnish the inn.

The dining room has an assortment of tables that seat two, four and six. Your hosts serve breakfast buffet style via little wicker trays, while you sit and bird or golfer watch. Wintergreen's 17th hole is in perfect view. There's a piano for guests who wish to plunk out their favorite tunes. Two chocolate retrievers will keep you company, if you bid them welcome.

A full breakfast comes with lodging. There are nine places to lunch nearby that do not require reservations. Trillium House generally serves dinner on Friday and Saturday evenings. Dinner reservations are necessary for Trillium as well as for several other choices within the resort. While dress is casual, you need to realize that temperatures are often 20 degrees cooler than the lower elevations.

The surrounding Wintergreen Resort offers you 10,000 prime acres of natural beauty, more than half left permanently intact. Some excellent downhill skiing is to be had there during the winter months, golfing in the non-snow seasons. Wintergreen's tennis ranks among the best in the nation. In addition to these sports, you can journey up and down 20 miles of hiking trails and overlooks, mapped and graded by degree of difficulty. A health spa with indoor and outdoor swimming, English riding, shopping and eating are other things to do at Wintergreen.

Trillium will help you make golf tee times, tennis court and riding reservations prior to your arrival.

Nearby points of interest include Ash Lawn, Woodrow Wilson's birthplace, Monticello and colleges galore: University of Virginia, James Madison, Virginia Military Institute, Washington and Lee, Sweetbriar, Mary Baldwin, Randolph Macon Women's College, and Bridgewater. Crabtree Falls is one of America's spectacular spots of picturesque scenery.

Close by is the Skyline Drive that merges into the Blue Ridge Parkway at Afton Mountain. The real treat coming to Trillium is by the ultimate scenic route, the Blue Ridge Parkway. At Reeds Gap between Milepost 13 and 14 you turn east onto Rt. 664 for one mile to the Wintergreen entry.

You are one hour from Charlottesville or Lynchburg and three hours from Washington, D. C., if you want to sightsee their offerings.

*P.O. Box 280*
*Nellysford, VA 22958*
*800/325-9126*

*From I-64 west to Exit 20 (Crozet). Rt. 250 west to Rt. 6, turn left. Follow 6 to 151 south 14 miles, turn right onto 664, go 4.5 miles. From entry gate to Wintergreen follow Wintergreen Drive 2 1/2 miles up the mountain; as you level off, Trillium will be on left.*

*Reservations confirmed with deposit of one night or half total stay, within 7 days of date. Refunds if cancellation received 14 days prior to arrival. Arrivals expected before 10 p. m.*

# COUNTRY FARE
*Nostalgic Blend of Yesteryear*

With an attractive facade, this small-town B&B sits along Route 11, the historic Lee Highway. Once well-traveled, the highway sees less traffic because hurrying motorists now take nearby Interstate 81, which parallels Route 11 nearby. Route 11 is a tourist's delight. It's well worth coming off I-81 and leisurely motoring the older road because it is teeming with significant points of interest from the Shenandoah Valley's past.

Immaculately restored, Country Fare was built in the late 18th century. An addition was built in 1840. From 1861 to 1864 the building served as a hospital. A half acre of magnificent magnolias, boxwoods and Japanese cherry trees encircle the home.

Your choice of rooms includes a spacious master bedroom with private shower, a room with twin beds and a Boston rocker, and a double with its own fireplace. The rooms have been hand-stenciled in original designs and are furnished with antiques and country collectibles.

Rates include a continental breakfast. You can eat homemade breads by the crackling fire in the common room. A brick patio provides a nice place to roost. An old log cabin, the original dwelling on the grounds, was an auction house for many years.

Proprietor Bette Hallgren is anxious to please her guests. You will find her old-fashioned hospitality a satisfying contrast to the hardness of today's world.

You will want to walk into the village of Woodstock. There are restaurants, shops and the ubiquitous historical markers. The town's charter was presented to the Virginia House of Burgesses on March 31, 1761, by a then-young representative named George Washington. He knew the area well because he had surveyed much of the Shenandoah Valley. From the town emanated the 8th Regiment during the Revolutionary War. The courthouse was designed by Thomas Jefferson in 1792 and today is a treasured national landmark because it is the oldest building of its kind still in use west of the Blue Ridge Mountains.

There is no end of things to do in the area. You have the Shenandoah National Park and Skyline Drive, New Market Battlefield, Belle Grove Plantation, Fishers Hill, July Shenandoah Music Festival, Luray and Shenandoah caverns, Apple Blossom Festival in Winchester, vineyards, hunting (deer, turkey, quail), antiquing, country auctions, craft fairs, bass and trout fishing, skiing in season, Wayside Theater and the August Shenandoah County Fair.

*402 North Main St.*
*Woodstock, VA 22664*
*703/459-4828*

*Take I-81 to Woodstock exit.*
*Take Rt. 42 to Rt. 11 north.*
*Call for reservations.*

# GOOD INTENT
*Relax or Tour*

You won't find a more back country road than where the 1890 farmhouse called "Good Intent" rests. And yet it's convenient to Interstate 81.

The white frame house with its old fashion picket fence welcomes you with cozy arms. Its pastoral setting totally relaxes you. If you want to shift into higher gear, you are positioned strategically for touring the Northern Shenandoah Valley.

Fran and Woody Rohrbaugh operate the B & B. Fran's grandfather built the home and her parents renovated it after World War II. After Woody retired from public school administration in Bucks County, Pa., and Fran from Educational Testing Service in Princeton, N.J., they moved to the place in 1975 and made some more improvements.

The house is furnished with antiques and family keepsakes. But that doesn't mean it's not comfortable. "We enjoy people," Fran smiles, "and that's why

we opened our home three years ago. We have a small business, just enough to be fun. We don't like to advertise but take whatever comes on its own."

Like other B & B owners, they have sampled a great many homes themselves, especially in England and Scotland. Fran has a pottery studio, where she makes dishes and serving pieces. They are for sale at Good Intent. She also puts up pear butter, pickles and other delectables from their garden. Woody, aptly named, makes wooden mirror frames! The couple is active in community services and art activities.

Twenty lush acres surround the home. Its location back off the road promises you tranquility. You look out at those wonderful mountains that parade down both sides of the Shenandoah Valley. For porch lovers there are a front porch swing and a large deck for sunning. For the energetic souls, there are lawn games and hiking.

Inside, guests can mill around the sitting room, which is equipped with TV.

A free country breakfast is served at the dining end of the country kitchen and might include preserves, biscuits, tomato juice — all homemade — and bacon or sausage and eggs to order, when you want them.

Nearby points of interest range from the Skyline Drive, New Market Battlefield Museum, Belle Grove Plantation, Strasburg and Woodstock museums to the Shenandoah Valley Music Festival in Orkney Springs and the caverns of Luray, Skyline and Shenandoah.

*Rt. 1, Box 435*
*Maurertown, VA 22644*
*703/459-2985*

*On Rt. 623, 6 miles northwest of Woodstock and 4 miles west of Maurertown. 30 miles south of Winchester. Reservations required, with $20 deposit. No refund for cancellation less than 3 days prior.*

# INN AT NARROW PASSAGE

*Endowed Setting*

Woodstock

Some of God's country is just more beautifully endowed than others, and this is one such setting. Apple orchards and vineyards surround this historic landmark against a backdrop of the Shenandoah River and Massanutten Mountain.

The Inn at Narrow Passage has been welcoming travelers since 1740 and is steeped in history. Settlers sought refuge from Indians here. It served as a stopover point for the stagecoach traffic along the old Valley Turnpike, once the trail of buffalo, then Indians, later the Wilderness Road for the pioneers, and now U.S. Route 11. Stonewall Jackson headquartered here during the Civil War's Shenandoah Valley Campaign. A boarding school for girls occupied the

quarters at one time, too.

The old log inn was built at a narrow passage along the famous trail, which parallels modern-day Interstate 81. Three miles from Woodstock, the passage itself is one of the most remarkable natural features in the region. Two streams, Narrow Passage Creek and the North Shenandoah River, are separated by a narrow ledge of limestone, just wide enough for the old roadway, now Route 11.

In 1983 Ed and Ellen Markel purchased the property and two years later had restored the inn to its Early American character. It is a perfect picture of the way you envision a colonial log inn. The original fireplaces are now operable and keep the inn cozy during the winter; they are throughout the com-

mon rooms and in some guest rooms. A massive limestone fireplace in the living room is a standout.

Twelve guest rooms have queen-sized beds and are furnished with antiques and colonial reproductions. Most have private baths and wood-burning fireplaces. Some feature canopy beds with crocheted tops and other such delicate treasures as double-wedding-ring quilts. Eighteenth century antiques and handmade reproductions are throughout the inn. Well-crafted, tin lighting fixtures hang in many rooms.

Breakfast comes with lodging, and you get to enjoy the hearty meal by fireside in a rustic, paneled dining room. Nice restaurants for other meals are close by.

A new addition gives conference

102

capabilities to the inn. Well-equipped and comfortable, the conference room, fireplace and all, is ideal for small, executive meetings and retreats during the week. The entire inn is air-conditioned for summertime comfort. Central heat will warm your non-fireplace side in the winter!

Large old trees skirt the fringe of the inn's setting amid five lush acres. In spring and summer, you revel in the fishing and rafting literally at your back door. Fall foliage beckons the hiker and the inn fills up fast. The George Washington National Forest covers much of the area. There are wineries, historic sites, caverns and antique shops to see. The Shenandoah Valley is a mecca of Civil War battlefields. During the winter, there is skiing at Massanutten and Bryce.

If you have come to the inn merely to rest some weary bones, then just sprawl out on the back porch and let the quietly flowing Shenandoah River untangle your thoughts.

The Markels and their three children will welcome you with down-home, family friendliness because they love sharing their colonial jewel of the past. The inn is one and a half hour's drive from Washington, D.C. Colonial times to perfection.

*U.S. 11 South*
*Woodstock, VA 22664*
*703/459-8000*

*Exit 72 off I-81. South on U.S. 11, Inn on left.*

*Check-in after 2 p.m. and before 9:30 p.m. Check-out 11 a.m.*

# SCHLISSELSMITH

*A Taste of Europe*

Innkeeper Pat Kollar frequently entertains nationally prominent figures and embassy guests from Washington, D.C. That tells you something about the hospitality! Not to mention the ease with which visitors from D.C. can get to Schlisselsmith — once they hit I-66 they never see a red light their entire way to the country inn.

Steven, a chef from Europe who speaks German and Hungarian, converses with his wife in German. They serve meals at their inn European-style, one course at a time. The informal dinner starts with an appetizer and soup, followed by homemade breads, salad, the main course of meat and vegetables, and a sinfully rich dessert. The *formal* dinner, a seven-course affair, is even more

elaborate and features authentic German dishes. Hostess Pat dresses in ethnic German attire. One of the best parts about dining is the eclectic set of silver flatware — you will see every Victorian pattern ever produced. Richly paneled walls trim the handsome dining room and make it a wonderful place for revelry. In good weather you may opt for breakfast on the veranda.

The country Victorian inn is in much demand for weddings, other special occasions and business meetings. It houses, decorates, feeds and entertains the whole wedding party and can serve up to 150 well-wishers at one of these galas.

A heated swimming pool is part of the complex. Bikes and badminton

equipment are also available. A double-sized, sunken whirlpool tub, encompassed by stained glass and greenery, may be reserved at an additional fee.

The elongated inn sits amid a backdrop of the Massanutten Mountain, just one and a half hours from D.C. In a most unique fashion, modern additions in 1981 and 1983 keep intact the Victorian appearance of the original building. Located on one of the famous Seven Bends of the Shenandoah River, the courtly Victorian mansion looks out to gorgeous mountain views of the George Washington National Forest.

You step back into the 1890s to partake of the ambience of Victoriana. But you do so with the modern-day convenience of such comforts as air conditioning, telephone and intercom. Selected antiques and a Franklin stove or 18th century fireplace set off each of the seven guest rooms. There are 12 fireplaces at Schlisselsmith! Most guests rooms have private baths and the larger suites adjoin sitting areas. The overall decor impresses you with a rich, satin look. European highlights lend a certain air to the interiors. The inn is one of the few providing for children. Young guests have access to a crib, small bed, games and bikes. They can also romp the inn's 26 acres.

If you choose to stray from the delights of the inn, you have the best of the Shenandoah Valley at your footsteps: New Market Battlefield and Civil War Museum; Massanutten, Bryce and Wintergreen ski resorts; Skyline Drive and Caverns, Luray and Shenandoah Caverns; Shenandoah Tri-Mountain Vineyards; Belle Grove Plantation; Wayside Theatre; Fishers Hill; and the many attractions in Winchester, historical and otherwise.                          ✔

*Rt. 1, Box 217 A1*
*Woodstock, VA 22664*

*Advance confirmed reservations essential. 72-hour notice with $20 service charge.*
*Three hours from Richmond or Baltimore. From D. C. take I-66 west to I-81. Exit 73 at Toms Brook; turn left and*
*go 1 mile to Rt. 11. Right on Rt. 11, through Toms Brook and Maurertown. Continue south to Pugh's Run; left on Rt. 663. Cross low-water bridge over Shenandoah River; Schlisselsmith is 1.2 miles on right.*

# THE COMMONWEALTH OF VIRGINIA

1. Alden
2. Amanda's
3. Anderson Cot.
4. Belle Grae
5. Bensonhouse of Richmond
6. Bensonhouse of Wmsbg.
7. Boxwood
8. Brookfield
9. Buckhorn
10. Caledonia
11. Catlin-Abbott
12. Chester
13. Clifton
14. Conyers
15. Country Fare
16. Edgewood
17. Fassifern
18. Fort Lewis
19. Foster-Harris
20. Fountain Hall
21. 4 & 20 Blackbirds
22. Frederick
23. Gay Street
24. Good Intent
25. Gristmill
26. Heritage

27. High Meadows
28. High Street
29. Historic Inns
30. Isle of Wight
31. Jordan Hollow Inn
32. L'Auberge Provencale
33. Manor at Taylor's Store
34. Martha Washington
35. Mary Bladon
36. Mayhurst
37. Meadow Lane
38. Memory House
39. Montross
40. Narrow Passage
41. Nichola
42. Norris House
43. Old Slave Quarters
44. Prospect Hill

45. Pumpkin House
46. Schlisselsmith
47. Silver Thatch
48. Sleepy Hollow
49. 200 South St.
50. Sycamore Hill
51. Thornrose
52. Trillium
53. Vine Cottage
54. Widow Kip's
55. Wmbg. Legacy

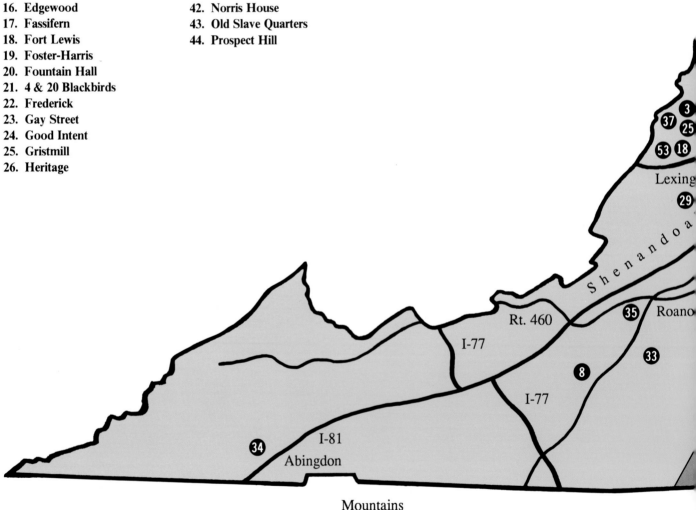

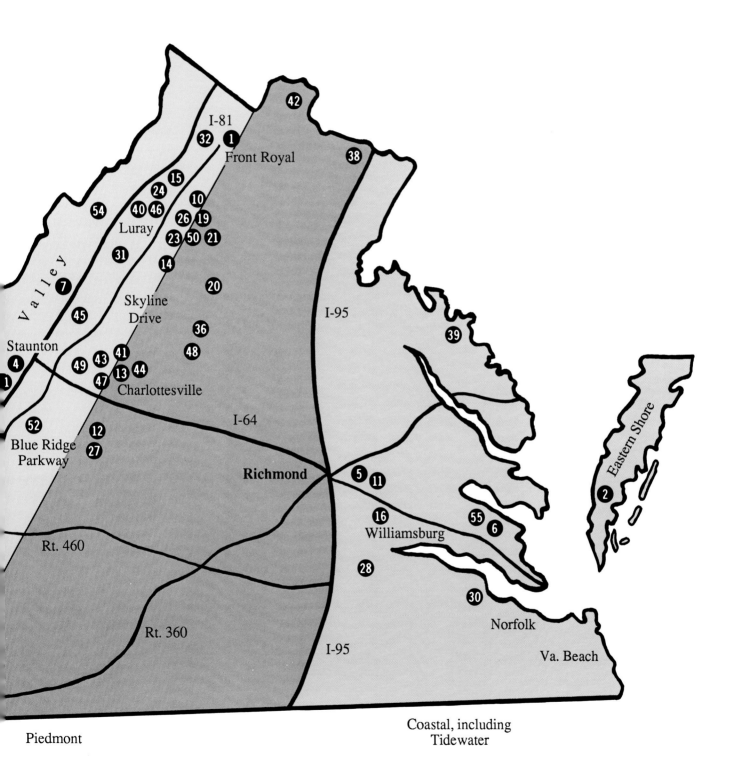

I-81

42

32 1

Front Royal

38

15

24

54

40 46

Luray

26 19

10

23 50 21

31

14

7

Skyline
Drive

20

45

36

Staunton

48

4

41

1

49 43

13 44

47

Charlottesville

I-64

52

I-95

12

27

39

Blue Ridge
Parkway

Richmond

5 11

Eastern Shore

16

2

Williamsburg

55 6

Rt. 460

28

30

Rt. 360

Norfolk

I-95

Va. Beach

Piedmont

Coastal, including
Tidewater

# Pictorial Cross-Reference:
## Costs, Services, and Amenities

| B&B OR INN/PAGE NO. | Credit cards | Discounts | Prices under $60 | Prices 60+ | Prices 100+ | Air conditioning | Antiques for sale | Bath, private | Common rooms | Conference rooms | Fans | Fireplaces | Musical instruments | Refrigerator use | Telephone in room | TV available | TV in room | Washer/dryer | Wheelchair access | Whirlpool | Young children welcomed | Pets welcomed | Smoking restrictions | Social drinking | Canoeing/rafting | Croquet | Fishing | Golf | Hiking | Horseback riding | Snow skiing | Swimming | Tennis | Shuttle transportation |
|---|---|---|---|---|---|---|---|---|---|---|---|---|---|---|---|---|---|---|---|---|---|---|---|---|---|---|---|---|---|---|---|---|---|---|
| Alden/33 | | | ● | | | ● | | | ● | | ● | | | | | | | | | | | | | ● | | | | | | | ● | | | |
| Amanda's/10 | | | | | ● | | | | | ● | | | | | | | | | ● | | | | ● | | ● | ● | | | | ● | | | ● | ● |
| Anderson Cot./78 | | | ● | | | | | ● | ● | | ● | ● | ● | ● | | ● | | | | | | | ● | | ● | ● | ● | | ● | | | | | |
| Belle Grae/72 | ● | ● | | ● | | | ● | ● | ● | | ● | ● | ● | | ● | ● | ● | ● | | ● | | | | ● | | ● | ● | | | | | ● | ● | ● |
| Bensonhouse of Richmond/58 | ● | | | ● | | | ● | ● | | | ● | | | ● | | | ● | ● | | | | | ● | | ● | ● | | | | | | | | |
| Bensonhouse of Wmsbg./94 | ● | | | ● | | ● | | ● | | ● | ● | | | ● | ● | | | | ● | | | | ● | | ● | ● | | | | | | | | |
| Boxwood/36 | | | ● | | | | ● | ● | | | ● | | ● | | ● | ● | | ● | | | | | | ● | | | | | ● | | | ● | ● | |
| Brookfield/32 | ● | | ● | | | ● | | ● | | | ● | ● | | ● | ● | ● | | ● | | | ● | | | | ● | | ● | | | | | | | |
| Buckhorn/28 | ● | ● | ● | | ● | | ● | | ● | | ● | ● | ● | | ● | | | ● | ● | | ● | ● | | ● | | ● | | | | | | | | |
| Caledonia/84 | ● | | | ● | | ● | | | ● | | ● | ● | | | ● | | | ● | | | | | ● | ● | ● | ● | ● | ● | ● | ● | ● | ● | ● | ● |
| Catlin-Abbott/60 | ● | | | ● | | ● | | | ● | | ● | | | ● | | | | ● | | | | | | ● | | | | | | | | | ● | |
| Chester/14 | | | | ● | | | ● | | | ● | | ● | | | | ● | | | | | | | | ● | | | | | ● | ● | | | ● | |
| Clifton/16 | ● | | | | | ● | ● | ● | | | ● | ● | | | ● | ● | | | ● | | | | | ● | | | | | ● | ● | | ● | ● | |
| Conyers/68 | | ● | | ● | | | ● | | ● | ● | ● | ● | | ● | | | | | | | | | ● | | | | | ● | ● | ● | | | ● | |
| Country Fare/100 | ● | | | ● | | | ● | | ● | | | | | ● | | | | | | | | | ● | | ● | | | | | | | | ● | |
| Edgewood/12 | ● | ● | | ● | | ● | ● | ● | ● | | ● | ● | | | | | | | | | | | ● | | ● | | | | | | | ● | | |
| Fassifern/42 | ● | ● | | ● | | ● | | | ● | | | | | ● | | | | | | | | | ● | | | | ● | | ● | | | ● | ● | |
| Fort Lewis/48 | ● | ● | ● | | | ● | | | ● | | ● | | | ● | | | | | | | | | ● | | | | | ● | ● | | | ● | | |
| Foster-Harris/86 | ● | | | ● | | ● | | | ● | | ● | | | ● | ● | | | | | | | | ● | | | | | | | | | | | ● |
| Fountain Hall/30 | ● | ● | | ● | | ● | ● | ● | ● | | ● | ● | | | | | | | | | | | ● | | | | | | ● | | | | | |
| 4 & 20 Blackbirds/8 | | | | | | ● | | ● | | | ● | | | | | | | | | | | | ● | | | ● | | | | | | | | |
| Frederick/74 | ● | ● | ● | | | | | ● | | | ● | | ● | | | | | | ● | ● | | | ● | | | ● | ● | | | | | | ● | |
| Gay Street/87 | | | | ● | | | ● | | ● | | ● | ● | | ● | ● | | | | | | | | ● | | ● | ● | ● | | | | | | | |
| Good Intent/101 | | | ● | | | | | ● | | | ● | | ● | | | ● | | | | | ● | | ● | | | | | | ● | | | | | |
| Gristmill/82 | ● | ● | ● | ● | | | ● | ● | ● | ● | ● | | ● | | | ● | | | ● | | | | ● | ● | | | | | ● | ● | ● | ● | ● | ● |
| Heritage/88 | ● | | | ● | | | ● | | ● | ● | ● | ● | | | | | | | ● | ● | ● | | ● | | ● | ● | | ● | | | ● | | | |
| High Meadows/20 | | ● | | | | ● | | | ● | | ● | ● | | ● | ● | | | ● | | ● | | | ● | | | ● | ● | | ● | | | ● | | |
| High Street/56 | ● | | ● | ● | | ● | | | ● | | ● | | | ● | | ● | | | | | | ● | | | | ● | | | | | | | | |
| Historic Inns/44 | ● | | | | | ● | | ● | | ● | | ● | | ● | ● | ● | ● | ● | | | ● | | | ● | | | ● | | | | | ● | ● | |
| Isle of Wight/66 | ● | ● | ● | | | | | ● | ● | | ● | | | ● | | ● | ● | | ● | ● | | | ● | | | | ● | | | | | | | |
| Jordan Hollow Inn/70 | ● | | | ● | | ● | | | ● | | ● | | | ● | | ● | | | | | | | ● | | ● | ● | | ● | ● | ● | | | ● | |
| L'Auberge Provencale/92 | ● | | | | ● | ● | | ● | | | ● | | | ● | | | | | | | | | ● | | | | | | | | | | | ● |
| Manor at Taylor's Store/64 | ● | ● | | ● | | ● | | ● | ● | | ● | | | | ● | | | | | | | | ● | | ● | | ● | | ● | | | | ● | ● |
| Martha Washington/6 | ● | ● | | ● | | ● | | ● | | | ● | | | | | | | | | | | | ● | ● | | | | | | | | ● | | ● |
| Mary Bladon/62 | ● | ● | ● | | | ● | | | ● | | ● | | | | ● | | | | | | | | ● | | | | | | | | | | | |
| Mayhurst/54 | ● | ● | | ● | | ● | ● | | ● | | ● | | | | | | | | | | | | ● | | | | | | | | | | | |
| Meadow Lane/79 | ● | | | | | | | | ● | | ● | | ● | | | | | | ● | | | | ● | | ● | ● | ● | | ● | ● | | | ● | |
| Memory House/9 | ● | | | ● | | | ● | | ● | | | | ● | | | ● | | | | | | | ● | | | | | | | | | | | ● |
| Montross/50 | ● | ● | | ● | | ● | | | ● | | ● | | | | ● | | | | | | ● | | ● | | | | | | | | | | ● | |
| Narrow Passage/102 | ● | | | ● | | ● | | ● | ● | | ● | | | | ● | | | | | | | | ● | | | ● | ● | | ● | | ● | ● | ● | |
| Nichola/18 | ● | | | ● | | ● | | | ● | | | | | | ● | | | | | | | | ● | | | | | | | | | | ● | |
| Norris House/40 | | | ● | ● | ● | ● | | | ● | | ● | ● | | | ● | | | | | | | | ● | | | | | | | | | | | |
| Old Slave Quarters/19 | ● | | | ● | ● | ● | | | ● | | ● | | ● | | | ● | | | | | | | ● | | | | | | | | | | | |
| Prospect Hill/22 | ● | | | ● | | ● | | | ● | | ● | | | | ● | | | | | | ● | ● | ● | | | | | | | | | ● | | |
| Pumpkin House/52 | ● | ● | ● | | | | ● | ● | ● | | ● | ● | | ● | | | | ● | | | | | ● | | ● | ● | | ● | | | ● | ● | ● | |
| Schlisselsmith/104 | | | ● | | | ● | | ● | | | ● | | ● | | | ● | | ● | | | | | ● | | ● | | | ● | | | ● | | ● | ● |
| Silver Thatch/24 | ● | ● | | ● | | ● | | | ● | | ● | | | | ● | | ● | | | | | | ● | | | | ● | | | | | | ● | ● |
| Sleepy Hollow/34 | ● | ● | | ● | | ● | | | ● | | | | ● | ● | ● | | ● | | | | | | ● | | ● | ● | | ● | ● | | | ● | ● | ● |
| 200 South St./26 | ● | ● | | ● | | ● | | | ● | | ● | | | ● | | | | | ● | ● | | | ● | | | | | | | | | ● | | |
| Sycamore Hill/90 | ● | | | ● | ● | ● | | | ● | | ● | | | | | | | | | ● | | | ● | | | | | | ● | | | ● | ● | |
| Thornrose/76 | | | ● | | | | | | ● | | | | | | ● | | | | | | | | ● | | | | | | ● | | | ● | ● | |
| Trillium/98 | | | ● | | | ● | | ● | | | ● | | | | ● | | | | ● | ● | | | ● | | | | | | ● | | | ● | ● | |
| Vine Cottage/38 | ● | | ● | | | | | | ● | | | ● | | | ● | | | | | | | | ● | | | | | | ● | | | ● | | |
| Widow Kip's/53 | ● | ● | ● | | | ● | | ● | ● | | ● | | | ● | | ● | | | | | | | ● | | | | | | ● | | ● | | | |
| Wmbg. Legacy/96 | ● | ● | | ● | | ● | | | ● | | ● | | | ● | | ● | | ● | | | | | ● | | ● | ● | | | ● | | | ● | ● | |

**KEY**

Verify with B&B if any minimum stay and if open year-round.
Prices are as of 1988 and apply to 2 guests sharing a room.
Bath may not be private for all rooms; check.

Fireplace means "working" and in some bedrooms.
Recreation marked if only on property or immediately accessible.
Always mention *Bed & Breakfast & Unique Inns* when making reservations!

# COMPREHENSIVE INDEX

*360 Virginia B&B's and Inns*

*There are many fine establishments listed here, some known to us but many we have not visited. We encourage you to write for information and talk with the innkeepers to be sure their facilities meet your needs and expectations.*

**The Comprehensive Index is copyright © 1988. It may not be reproduced or copied in any manner.**

## ABINGDON
Litchfield Hall
247 East Valley St.
Abingdon, VA 24210
703/628-9317

Maplewood Farm
Rt. 7, Box 272
Abingdon, VA 24210
703/628-2640

Martha Washington Inn
P.O. Box 1037
Abingdon, VA 24210
703/628-3161

Mason Place
243 Mason Place, NW
Abingdon, VA 24210
703/628-2887

Summerfield Inn
101 West Valley St.
Abingdon, VA 24210
703/628-5905

## ACCOMAC
The Twyford Family B&B
Mt. Curtis St.
Accomac, VA 23301
804/787-3807

## ALDIE
Little River Inn
Box 116
Aldie, VA 22001
703/327-6742

## ALEXANDRIA
Alexandria Lodgings
10 Sunset Dr.
Alexandria, VA 22313
703/836-5575

The Little House
719 Gibbon St.
Alexandria, VA 22314
703/548-9654

Morrison House
116-S. Alfred St.
Alexandria, VA 22313
800/367-0800

Old Colony Inn
625 First St.
Alexandria, VA 22314
703/548-6300

## AMISSVILLE
Bunree B&B
Amissville, VA 22002
804/381-5779 weeknights

Four & Twenty
Blackbirds B&B
P.O. Box 95
Amissville, VA 22002
703/937-5885

## ARLINGTON
Carter B&B
1041 North Stafford St.
Arlington, VA 22201
703/525-7192

Crystal B&B
2620 South Fern St.
Arlington, VA 22202
703/548-7652

Memory House
6404 N. Washington Blvd.
Arlington, VA 22205
703/534-4607

## BANCO
Olive Mill B&B Inn
Banco, VA 22711
703/923-4664

## BASSETT
Annie's Country Inn
Rt. 5, Box 562
Bassett, VA 24055
703/629-1517

## BASYE
Sky Country Inn
P.O. Box 80
Basye, VA 22810
703/856-2147

## BATESVILLE
Westbury
Batesville, VA 22924
804/979-7264

## BEDFORD
The Bedford House
422 Avenel Ave.
Bedford, VA 24523
703/586-5050

The Longwood Inn
517 Longwood Ave.
Bedford, VA 24523
703/586-2282

Mt. Spring Farm B&B
Rt. 4, Box 45
Bedford, VA 24523
703/586-4929

Otter's Den
Rt. 2, Box 160E
Bedford, VA 24523
703/586-2204

## BERRYVILLE
Rocks & Rills
Rt. 2, Box 3895
Berryville, VA 22611
703/955-1246

## BLACKSBURG
Bea's B&B
702 Crestwood Dr.
Blacksburg, VA 24060
703/961-0472

## BLUEGRASS —
see Monterey

## BOSTON
Meadowood
P.O. Box 29
Boston, VA 22713
703/547-3851

## BOWLING GREEN
The Old Mansion
Box 835
Bowling Green, VA 22427
804/633-5781

## BOYCE
The River House
Rt. 2, Box 135
Boyce, VA 22620
703/837-1476

## BRIDGEWATER
Bear & Dragon B&B
401 N. Main St.
Bridgewater, VA 22812
703/828-2807

## BUMPASS
Rockland Farm Retreat
P.O. Box 118
Bumpass, VA 23024
703/895-5098

## BURKEVILLE
Hyde Park Farm
Rt. 2, Box 38
Burkeville, VA 23922
804/645-8431

## CAPE CHARLES
Henrietta's Cottage
613 Tazewell Ave.
Cape Charles, VA 23310

Nottingham Ridge
P.O. Box 97-B
Cape Charles, VA 23310
804/331-1010

Pickett's Harbor B&B
P.O. Box 97AA
Cape Charles, VA 23310
804/221-2212

Sea Gate B&B
9 Tazewell Ave.
Cape Charles, VA 23310
804/331-2206

Stratton Manor
Box 289
Cape Charles, VA 23310
804/331-1992

## CAPRON
The Kitchens
Rt. 1, Box 55
Capron, VA 23829
804/658-4381

Sandy Hill Farm B&B
Rt. 1, Box 55
Capron, VA 23829
804/658-4381

## CHARLES CITY
Edgewood Plantation
Rt. 2, Box 490
Charles City, VA 23030
804/829-2962

## CHARLOTTESVILLE AREA
Aldeman House
804/979-7264

Auburn Hill
804/979-7264

Bellair
804/979-7264

Belleview
804/979-7264

Ben-Coolyn
804/979-7264

Blenheim Claim House
804/979-7264

Bollingwood Place
804/979-7264

Brooksville
804/979-7264

Brookwood
804/979-7264

Burnley
804/979-7264

Canterbury
804/979-7264

Carrickfergus
804/979-7264

Carrsbrook
804/979-7264

Chathill
804/979-7264

Chaumine
804/979-7264

Chester
Rt. 4, Box 57
Scottsville, VA 24590
804/286-3960

Clifton, The Country Inn
Rt. 9, Box 412
Charlottesville, VA 22901
804/286-3960

Coleman Cottage
804/971-1800

Copps Hill Farm
804/971-1800

Country Cottage
804/971-1800

Dogwood
804/797-7264

## CHARLOTTESVILLE
— cont.

Edgemont
804/797-7264

Ednam
804/797-7264

Felicity
804/797-7264

Harris House
804/797-7264

Heartsease
804/797-7264

Hessian
804/797-7264

High Meadows
Rt. 4, Box 6
Scottsville, VA 24590
804/286-2218

Hill Street
804/979-7264

Ingleside
804/979-7264

Ingwood
804/979-7264

Laurel Run
804/979-7264

Leeward
804/979-7264

Locust Hill
804/979-7264

Meadowbrook
804/979-7264

Meadowrun
804/979-7264

Nichola Log Cabin
804/979-7264

North Garden Cottage
804/979-7264

Old Ballard Road
804/979-7264

Old Slave Quarters
804/979-7264

Oxbridge Inn Guest House
316 14th St. NW
Charlottesville, VA 22903
804/295-7707

Peacock Hill
804/979-7264

The Prodigal
Scottsville, VA 24590
804/979-7264

Prospect Hill Inn
Rt. 3, Box 430
Trevilians, VA 23093
703/967-0844

Recoletta
804/979-7264

Robin Hill
804/979-7264

Schoolhouse Hill
804/979-7264

1740 House Antiques
Rt. 10, Box 114
Charlottesville, VA 22901
804/977-1740

Silver Thatch Inn
3001 Hollymead Rd.
Charlottesville, VA 22901
804/978-4686

Timberlake
804/979-7264

200 South Street Inn
200 South St.
Charlottesville, VA 22901
804/979-0200

Whippoorwill Farm
804/979-7264

Winston
804/979-7264

Wood Lane
804/979-7264

Woodstock Hall
Rt. 3, Box 40
Charlottesville, VA 22901
804/293-8977

## CHATHAM
Sims-Mitchell House
P.O. Box 846
Chatham, VA 24531
804/432-0595

## CHINCOTEAGUE
Assateague Inn
P.O. Box 1006
Chincoteague, VA 23336
804/336-3738

Channel Bass Inn
100 Church St.
Chincoteague, VA 23336
804/336-6148

The Little Traveller Inn
112 N. Main St.
Chincoteague, VA 23336
804/336-6686

Miss Molly's Inn
113 N. Main St.
Chincoteague, VA 23336
804/336-6686

Year of the Horse Inn
600 S. Main St.
Chincoteague, VA 23336
804/336-3221

## CHRISTIANSBURG
Coyle B&B
Rt. 1, Box 404
Christiansburg, VA 24073
703/382-6322

## CHURCH
Bensonhouse
804/648-7560

## CHURCHVILLE
Buckhorn Inn
Star Route, Box 139
Churchville, VA 24421
703/337-6900

## CLARKSVILLE
Needmore Inn
801 Virginia Ave.
Clarksville, VA 23927
804/374-2866

## CLUSTER SPRINGS
Oak Grove Plantation
P.O. Box 45
Cluster Springs, VA 24535
804/575-7137

## COLONIAL BEACH
Richard R. Bayliss
Colonial Beach, VA 22443
804/224-7595

## CULPEPER
Fountain Hall B&B
609 S. East St.
Culpeper, VA 22701-3222
703/825-6708

Stuartfield Hearth B&B
Rt.1, Box 199
Mitchells, VA 22729
703/825-8132

## DILLWYN
Buckingham Springs Plantation
Rt. 3, Box 176
Dillwyn, VA 23936
804/392-8770

## DUBLIN
Bell's B&B
Giles Ave.
Dublin, VA 24084
703/674-6331

## EARLYSVILLE
Copps Hill Farm
Earlysville, VA 22936
804/979-7264

Polaris Farm
Earlysville, VA 22936
804/979-7264

## EASTHAM
Maho-No-Yama
804/979-7264

## EDINBURG
Mary's Country Inn
Rt. 2, Box 4
Edinburg, VA 22824
703/984-8286

## ELKTON —
see Harrisonburg

## EMPORIA
105 1/2 B&B
105 Goodwyn St.
Emporia, VA 23847
804/634-2590

## FANCY GAP
Cascades Mountain Inn
Rt. 2
Fancy Gap, VA 24328
703/728-2300

## FARMVILLE
The Lanscott House
Victorian B&B
408 High St.
Farmville, VA 23901
703/392-4317

## FLINT HILL —
see Washington

## FLOYD
Brookfield Inn
P.O. Box 341
Floyd, VA 24091
703/763-3363

## FREDERICKSBURG
Bensonhouse of Fredericksburg
804/648-7560

Kenmore Inn
1200 Princess Anne St.
Fredericksburg, VA 22401
703/371-7622

La Vista Plantation
Rt. 3, Box 1255
Fredericksburg, VA 22401
703/898-8444

McGrath House
225 Princess Anne St.
Fredericksburg, VA 22401
703/371-4363

Richard Johnson Inn
711 Caroline St.
Fredericksburg, VA 22401
703/899-7506

## FRONT ROYAL
Alden Inn
35 N. Royal Ave.
Front Royal, VA 22630
703/636-6645

Constant Spring Inn
413 S. Royal Ave.
Front Royal, VA 22630
703/635-7010

## GLASGOW
Balcony Downs Country Inn
P.O. Box 563
Glasgow, VA 24555
703/258-2100

## GOOCHLAND COURT
Evangeline
Goochland Court, VA 23063
804/979-7264

## GORDONSVILLE
Ridge Top Country Cottage
Gordonsville, VA 22942
703/832-2946

Sleepy Hollow Farm
Rt. 3, Box 43
Gordonsville, VA 22942
703/832-5555

## GORE
Rainbow's End
Rt. 1, Box 335
Gore, VA 22637
703/858-2808

## GREENWOOD
Coleman Cottage
Greenwood, VA 22943
804/979-7264

## HAMILTON
Hamilton Garden Inn
353 W. Colonial Highway Rt. 7
Hamilton, VA 22068
703/338-3693

## HARRISONBURG
Boxwood
Rt.1, Box 130
Hinton, VA 22831
703/867-5772

Joanne's B&B
Rt.2, Box 276
Elkton, VA 22827
703/298-9723

Kingsway B&B
3581 Singers Glen Rd.
Harrisonburg, VA 22801
703/867-9696

Pumpkin House
Rt. 2, Box 155
Mt. Crawford, VA 22841
703/434-6963

## HAYWOOD
Shenandoah Springs
    Country Inn
Box 122
Haywood, VA 22722
703/923-4300

## HEATHSVILLE
Belleville B&B
P.O. Box 274
Heathsville, VA 22473
804/580-5293

## HIGHLAND
Colonial Pine Inn
Box 2309 Hickory St.
Highland, VA 24444
703/526-2060

## HILLSVILLE
Tipton House B&B
1043 N. Main St.
Hillsville, VA 24343
703/728-2351

## HINTON —
see Harrisonburg

## HOT SPRINGS
Vine Cottage Inn
P.O. Box 918
Hot Springs, VA 24445
703/839-2422

## HOWARDSVILLE
Fish Pond Plantation
Rt. 1, Box 48
Howardsville, VA 24562
804/263-4484

## IRVINGTON
King Carter Inn
P.O. Box 425
Irvington, VA 22480
804/438-6053

## KESWICK
Olde Poorhouse Farm
Keswick, VA 22947
804/979-7264

## LANCASTER
Greenvale Manor
Lancaster, VA 22503
804/462-5995

The Inn at Levelfields
P.O. Box 216
Lancaster, VA 22503
804/435-6887

## LEESBURG
Carradoc Hall
Rt. 7
Leesburg, VA 22075
703/771-9200

Colonial Inn of Leesburg
19 South King St.
Leesburg, VA 22075
703/777-5000

Cummings Family
145 Lincoln
Leesburg, VA 22075
703/836-7997

Fleetwood Farm
Rt. 1, Box 306-A
Leesburg, VA 22075
703/327-4325

Laurel Brigade Inn
20 W. Market St.
Leesburg, VA 22075
703/777-1010

Norris House Inn
108 Loudoun St., SW
Leesburg, VA 22075
703/777-1806

## LEXINGTON
Alexander-Withrow House
3 W. Washington St.
Lexington, VA 24450
703/463-2044

Fassifern
RFD 5, Box 87
Lexington, VA 24450
703/463-1013

Historic Country Inns
11 N. Main St.
Lexington, VA 24450
703/463-2044

Llewellyn Lodge B&B
603 S. Main St.
Lexington, VA 24450
703/463-3235

Maple Hall
U.S. Rt. 11
Lexington, VA 24450
703/463-2044

McCampbell Inn
11 N. Main St.
Lexington, VA 24450
703/463-2044

McCormick House
220 W. Washington St.
Lexington, VA 24450
703/463-3247

Nichols House
106 McDowell St.
Lexington, VA 24450
703/463-5227

## LINCOLN
Oakland Green
Box 154
Lincoln, VA 22078
703/338-7628

## LURAY
Boxwood Place
120 High St.
Luray, VA 22835
703/743-4748

Jordan Hollow Farm Inn
Rt. 2, Box 375
Stanley, VA 22851
703/778-2209

Mountain View House
151 S. Court St.
Luray, VA 22835
703/743-3723

The Ruffner House
Luray, VA 22835
703/743-7855

Shenandoah Countryside
Rt. 2, Box 377
Luray, VA 22835
703/743-6434

Shenandoah River Roost B&B
Rt. 3, Box 224B
Luray, VA 22835
703/743-3467

## MATHEWS
Ravenwood Inn
P.O. Box 250
Mathews, VA 23109-0250
804/725-7272

Riverfront House, B&B
Rt. 41 East, Box 319
Mathews, VA 23109
804/725-9975

Cedar Point Farm Country Inn
P.O. Box 369
Mathews, VA 23109
804/725-9535

## MAURERTOWN —
see Woodstock

## McGAHEYSVILLE
Shenandoah Valley Farm & Inn
Rt. 1, Box 142
McGaheysville,VA 22840
703/289-5402

## MECHANICSVILLE —
see Richmond

## MITCHELLS —
see Culpeper

## MIDDLEBURG
Brier Patch At Middleburg
P.O. Box 803
Middleburg, VA 22117
703/327-4455

Luck House
P.O. Box 919
Middleburg, VA 22117
703/687-5387

McConnell House
P.O. Box 385
Middleburg, VA 22117
703/687-6301

Red Fox Inn
P.O. Box 385
Middleburg, VA 22117
703/687-6301

Welbourne
State Rd. 743
Welbourne, Middleburg, VA 22117
703/687-3201

Windsor House Rest
& Country Inn
Box 1400
Middleburg, VA 22117
703/687-6800

## MIDDLETOWN
Wayside Inn Since 1797
7783 Main St.
Middletown, VA 22645
703/869-1797

## MILLBORO
Fort Lewis Lodge
Millboro, VA 24460
703/925-2314

Nimrod Hall
Star Rt. 8, Box 31
Millboro, VA 24460

## MOLLUSK
Greenville Manor
Box 174
Mollusk, VA 22517
804/462-5995

## MONETA
Holland-Duncan House
Rt. 3, Box 681
Moneta, VA 24121
703/721-8510

## MONTEREY
Blue Grass B&B
Star Rt. B, Box 20
Blue Grass, VA 24413
703/474-3297

Bobbie's B&B
Star Rt. C, Box 5
Monterey, VA 24465
703/468-2308

Highland Inn
P.O. Box 40
Monterey, VA 24465
703/468-2143

## MONTROSS
Inn at Montross
P.O. Box 908
Montross, VA 22520
804/493-9097

## MT. CRAWFORD —
see Harrisonburg

## MT. HOLLY
Mt. Holly House
P.O. Box 130
Mt. Holly, VA 22524
804/472-3336

## MT. JACKSON
Sky Chalet
Star Rt. 28
Mt. Jackson, VA 22842
703/856-2147

Widow Kip's Country Inn
Box 117, Rt. 1
Mt. Jackson, VA 22842
703/477-2400

## MT. SIDNEY
The Pittance Inn
P.O. Box 165
Mt. Sidney, VA 24467
703/248-2710

## NATURAL BRIDGE
Burger's Country Inn
Rt. 2, Box 564
Natural Bridge, VA 24578
703/291-2464

## NELLYSFORD —
see Wintergreen

## NEWBERN
Valley Pike Inn
Newbern, VA 24126
703/674-1810

## NEW MARKET
Susie Q Farm
New Market, VA 22844
703/896-9702

## NEWPORT
The Newport House
Rt. 2, Box 561-E
Newport, VA 24128

## NORFOLK
B&B Larchmont
1112 Buckingham Ave.
Norfolk, VA 23508
804/489-8449

Cameron Residence
1605 Bill St.
Norfolk, VA 23518
804/587-0673

## OCCOQUAN
Rockledge 1758
Occoquan, VA 22125
703/690-3370

## ONANCOCK
Onanock Manor Inn
84 Market St.
Onanock, VA 23417
804/787-3521

## ORANGE
Five Oaks Farm, B&B
Rt. 2, Box 427
Orange, VA 22960
703/854-5934

The Hidden Inn
249 Caroline St.
Orange, VA 22960
703/672-3625

Mayhurst Inn
P.O. Box 707
Orange, VA 22960
703/672-5597

Shadows
Rt. 20
Orange, VA 22960

Willow Grove Plantation
Rt. 5 N.
Orange, VA 22960

**ORLEAN**
Hilltop Manor
Rt. 688, Box 36
Orlean, VA 22128
703/364-3292

**PARIS**
The Ashby Inn
Rt. 1, Box 2A
Paris, VA 22130
703/592-3900

**PETERSBURG**
High Street Inn
405 High St.
Petersburg, VA 23803
804/733-0505

Mayfield Inn
P.O. Box 2265
Petersburg, VA 23804
804/733-0866

**QUICKSBURG**
McCoy's Mill
Rt. 1, Box 94
Quicksburg, VA 22847
703/740-8943

**RADFORD**
Central Depot
301 First St.
Radford, VA 24141
703/639-9000

**RESTON**
M Malishenko, B&B
11610 Newbridge Ct.
Reston, VA 22091
703/860-5513

**RICHMOND**
Abbie Hill B&B
2216 Monument Ave.
Richmond, VA 23220
804/353-4656

Bensonhouse Richmond
804/648-7560

The Catlin-Abbott House
2304 E. Broad St.
Richmond, VA 23223
804/780-3746

Hanover Hosts in the Fan
P.O. Box 25145
Richmond, VA 23220
804/355-5855

James Branch Cabell House
3201 Monument Ave.
Richmond, VA 23221
804/355-5959

Mechanicsville
Battlefield House
804/648-7560

**ROANOKE**
The Country Inn
6910 Williamson Rd., NW
Roanoke, VA 24019
703/366-1987

The Manor at Taylor's Store
Rt. 1, Box 533
Wirtz, VA 24184
703/721-3951

The Mary Bladon House
381 Washington Ave., SW
Roanoke, VA 24016
703/344-5361

**ROUND HILL**
Round Hill Hall
Box 14, RR 1
Round Hill, VA 22141
703/338-9221

**SALEM**
The Old Manse B&B
530 E. Main St.
Salem, VA 24153
703/389-3921

**SMITHFIELD**
Isle of Wight Inn
1607 S. Church St.
Smithfield, VA 23430
804/357-3176

Smithfield Station
415 S. Church St.
Smithfield, VA 23430
804/357-7700

**SCOTTSVILLE —
see Charlottesville**

**SPERRYVILLE**
The Conyers House
Slate Mills Rd.
Sperryville, VA 22740
703/987-8025

Nethers Mill
Rt. 1, Box 62
Sperryville, VA 22740
703/987-8625

**SPRINGFIELD**
The Stead Family
7136 Rolling Forest Ave.
Springfield, VA 22152
703/451-2642

**STANDARDSVILLE**
Golden Horseshoe Inn
Rt. 33 W.
Standardsville, VA 22973
804/985-2740

**STANLEY —
see Luray**

**STAUNTON**
Belle Grae Inn
515 W. Frederick St.
Staunton, VA 24401
703/886-5151

Frederick House
P.O. Box 1387
Staunton, VA 24401
703/885-4220

Lambsgate B&B
Rt. 1, Box 63
Swoope, VA 24479
703/337-6929

Thornrose House At Gypsy
Hill
531 Thornrose Ave.
Staunton, VA 24401
703/885-7026

**STEELE'S TAVERN**
Osceola Mill Country Inn
Rt. 56
Steele's Tavern, VA 24476
703/377-MILL

**STRASBURG**
Hotel Strasburg
201 Holliday St.
Strasburg, VA 22657
703/465-9191

**SWOOPE —
see Staunton**

**TANGIER**
Hilda Crockett's
    Chesapeake House
P.O. Box 194
Tangier, VA 23440
804/891-2331

Sunset Inn
Box 159
Tangier, VA 23440
804/891-2535

**SYRIA**
Graves Mountain Lodge
Rt. 670
Syria, VA 22743
703/923-4231

**TOWNSEND**
B&B of Pickett's Harbor
Box 96
Townsend, VA 23443
804/331-2212

**TREVILIANS —
see Charlottesville**

**TROUTDALE**
Fox Hill Inn
P.O. Box 88
Troutdale, VA 24378
703/677-3313

**UPPERVILLE**
Gibson Hall Inn
P.O. Box 225, Rt. 50
Upperville, VA 22176
703/592-3514

1763 Inn
Rt. 1, Box 19D
Upperville, VA 22176
703/592-3848

**URBANNA**
The Town House
1880 Prince George St., Box 757
Urbanna, VA 23175
804/758-3521

**VESUVIUS**
Irish Gap Inns
Rt. 1, Box 40
Vesuvius, VA 24483
804/922-7701

Sugar Tree Inn Ltd.
Hwy. 56
Vesuvius, VA 24483
703/377-2197

**VIRGINIA BEACH**
Angie's Guest Cottage
302 24th St.
Virginia Beach, VA 23451
804/428-4690

The Grater's Residence
209 Great Meadows Ct.
Virginia Beach, VA 23452
804/486-4982

Matuck
4501 Ocean Front Ave.
Virginia Beach, VA 23451

The Picket Fence
209 43rd St.
Virginia Beach, VA 23451
804/428-8861

**WACHAPREAGUE**
The Burton House
11 Brooklyn St., P.O. Box 182
Wachapreague, VA 23480
804/787-4560

**WARM SPRINGS**
Anderson Cottage
Box 176
Warm Springs, VA 24484
703/839-2975

The Inn at Gristmill Square
Box 359
Warm Springs, VA 24484
703/839-2231

Meadow Lane Lodge
Star Rt. A, Box 110
Warm Springs, VA 24484
703/839-5959

Three Hills Inn
P.O. Box 99
Warm Springs, VA 24484
703/839-5381

**WARRENTON**
Rosemont Farm Inn
Rt. 3. Box 240
Warrenton, VA 22186
703/347-5422

**WARSAW**
Greenwood
Rt. 2, Box 50
Warsaw, VA 22572
804/333-4353

**WASHINGTON**
Caledonia Farm
Rt. 1, Box 2080
Flint Hill, VA 22627
703/675-3693

Foster-Harris House
P.O. Box 333
Washington, VA 22747
703/675-3757

Gay Street Inn
P.O. Box 237
Washington, VA 22747
703/675-3288

Heritage House
P.O. Box 90
Washington, VA 22747
703/675-3207

The Inn at Little Washington
P.O. Box 300
Washington, VA 22747
703/675-3800

Sycamore Hill House
Rt. 1, Box 978
Washington, VA 22747
703/675-3046

**WATERFORD**
James Moore House
P.O. Box 161
Waterford, VA 22190
703/882-3342

The Pink House
Waterford, VA 22190
703/882-3453

**WHITE POST**
Dearmont Hall
Rt.1, Box 158A
White Post, VA 22663
703/837-1397

L'Auberge Provencale
P.O. Box 119
White Post, VA 22663
703/837-1375

**WICOMICO**
West End Plantation
Wicomico, VA 23184
804/648-7560

**WILLIAMSBURG**
Bensonhouse Williamsburg
804/648-7560

Brass Lantern Lodge
1782 Jamestown Rd.
Williamsburg, VA 23185
804/229-4320

Cant Hill Guest Home
4 Canterbury Ln.
Williamsburg, VA 23185
804/229-6623

Carter's Guest House
903 Lafayette St.
Williamsburg, VA 23184
804/229-1117

The Castles at Williamsburg
711 Goodwin St.
Williamsburg, VA 23185
804/220-9161

The Cedars
616 Jamestown Rd.
Williamsburg, VA 23185
804/229-3591

Chantilly
171 W. Queens Dr.
Williamsburg, VA 23185
804/229-3434

The Chateau
330 Indian Springs Rd.
Williamsburg, VA 23185
804/253-2323

Country Cottage of Williamsburg
701 Monumental Ave.
Williamsburg, VA 23185
804/229-6914

Dazley Guest House
494 Penniman Rd.
Williamsburg, VA 23187
804/253-0286

The Elms
708 Richmond Rd.
Williamsburg, VA 23685
804/229-1551

Fox Grape
701 Monumental Ave.
Williamsburg, VA 23185
804/229-6914

Governor's Trace
303 Capitol Landing Rd.
Williamsburg, VA 23185
804/229-7552

Himmelbed Guest House
706 Richmond Rd.
Williamsburg, VA 23185

Hites Guest House
704 Monumental Ave.
Williamsburg, VA 23185
804/229-4814

Hughes Guest Home
106 Newport Ave.
Williamsburg, VA 23187
804/229-3493

Johnson's Guest Home
101 Thomas Nelson Ln.
Williamsburg, VA 23185
804/229-3909

Liberty Rose Colonial B&B
1022 Jamestown Rd.
Williamsburg, VA 23185
804/253-1260

Pagen's Guest House
215 Tarleton Bivouac
Williamsburg, VA 23185
804/887-8034

The Spiggle Guest House
720 College Terrace
Williamsburg, VA 23187
804/253-0202

Thompson Guest House
1007 Lafayette St.
Williamsburg, VA 23185
804/229-3455

War Hill Inn
4560 Longhill Rd.
Williamsburg, VA 23185
804/565-0248

A Williamsburg Legacy
930 Jamestown Rd.
Williamsburg, VA 23185
804/220-0524

Williamsburg Sampler B&B
922 Jamestown Rd.
Williamsburg, VA 23185
804/253-0398

Wood's Guest House
1208 Steward Dr.
Williamsburg, VA 23185
804/229-3376

## WILLIS
Woodberry Inn
Rt. 3, Box 27
Willis, VA 24380
703/593-2567

## WINCHESTER
Northwest Trail Tourist Home
302 W. Boscowen St., Box 378
Winchester, VA 22601
703/662-0484

## WINTERGREEN
Rodes Farm Inn Wintergreen
Box 239
Wintergreen, VA 22938
804/361-1200

Trillium House
P.O. Box 280
Nellysford, VA 22958
800/325-9126

## WIRTZ —
see Roanoke

## WISE
The Inn At Wise Courthouse
P.O. Box 887
Wise, VA 24293
703/328-2251

## WOODSTOCK
Candlewick Inn
127 N. Church St.
Woodstock, VA 22664
703/459-8008

Country Fare
402 N. Main St.
Woodstock, VA 22664
703/459-4828

Good Intent
Rt. 1, Box 435
Maurertown, VA 22644
703/459-2985

Inn at Narrow Passage
P.O. Box 83
Woodstock, VA 22664
703/459-8000

Schlisselsmith
RFD 1, Box 217-A1
Woodstock, VA 22664
703/459-5369

## RESERVATION SERVICES

Amanda's B&B Resv. Ser.
1428 Park Ave.
Baltimore, MD 21217
301/225-0001

B&B League
3639 Van Ness St. NW
Washington, D.C. 20008
202/363-7767

B&B Ltd. Of D.C.
P.O. Box 12011
Washington, D.C. 20005
202/328-3510

B&B On the Hill
2304 E. Broad St.
Richmond, VA 23223
804/780-3746

B&B Registry
Michigan
612/646-4238

B&B Tidewater
P.O. Box 3343
Norfolk, VA 23514
804/627-1983

Bensonhouse
P.O. Box 15131
Richmond, VA 23227
804/648-7560

Blue Ridge B&B
Rt. 2, Box-3895
Berryville, VA 22611
703/955-1246

Commissioned Host & Toast, Inc.
7811 Lewinsville Rd.
McLean, VA 22102
703/847-5211

Guesthouses B&B, Inc.
P.O. Box 5737
Charlottesville, VA 22905
804/979-7264

Princely B&B, Ltd.
819 Prince St.
Alexandria, VA 22314
703/683-2159

Reservation Station
P.O. Box 8803
Roanoke, VA 24014
703/345-1801

Rockbridge Reservations
Sleepy Hollow
P.O. Box 76
Brownsburg, VA 24415
703/348-5698

Shenandoah Valley
B&B Reservations
P.O. Box 634
Woodstock, VA 22664
703/459-8241

So Journers B&B
Reservation Service
P.O. Box 3587
Lynchburg, VA 24503
804/384-1655

Sweet Dreams & Toast, Inc.
1525 D St. SE
Washington, D.C. 20003
202/483-9191

The Travel Tree
P.O. Box 838
Williamsburg, VA 23185
804/229-4037

**Dear Reader,**

Please feel free to send us your comments about the book and/or the establishments both pictured and listed. We are also interested in learning about other B&B's in Virginia and in neighboring states for future publications.

Direct comments to: Editor

Crystal Springs Publishing

P.O. Box 8814

Roanoke, VA 24014

# BED & BREAKFAST
and
# UNIQUE INNS
of VIRGINIA

# ORDER INFORMATION

**PHONE ORDERS 703/982-2029**

**SEND MAIL ORDERS TO:**

▰ Crystal Springs Publishing
Department B
P.O. Box 8814
Roanoke, Virginia 24014

When ordering, please submit the following information:

**Order Placed By: (please print)**

Name: _____

Address: _____

City/State/Zip: _____

☐ **VISA** # _____

☐ **MasterCard** # _____

☐ Check

**As Gift — Ship To: (please print)**

Name: _____

Address: _____

City/State/Zip: _____

From: _____

_____

| HOW MANY? | PRICE PER BOOK | TOTAL PRICE |
|---|---|---|
| | 15.95 | |
| SHIPPING | PER BOOK | TOTAL SHIPPING |
| | 2.00 | |
| TAX-VA RES. 4½% | PER BOOK | TOTAL TAX |
| | .72 | |
| TOTAL ORDER | PER BOOK | TOTAL ORDER |
| | 18.67 | |

FOR QUANTITIES OVER 5, PLEASE ORDER BY PHONE.
ALLOW 3 WEEKS DELIVERY.